FISHING

WITH

SIMON

Also by Charles Lynch

China, One Fourth of the World
You Can't Print THAT!
Our Retiring Prime Minister
Race for the Rose: Election 1984
A Funny Way to Run a Country
The Lynch Mob
Up from the Ashes: The Rideau Club Story

————————————

CHARLES LYNCH

FISHING
WITH
SIMON

PRENTICE HALL CANADA INC., SCARBOROUGH, ONTARIO

Canadian Cataloguing in Publication Data

Lynch, Charles, 1919-
  Fishing with Simon

ISBN 0-13-318809-4

1. Fishing   I Title.

SH441.L8 1991   799.1'2   C91-094467-9

Prentice-Hall Inc., *Englewood Cliffs, New Jersey*
Prentice-Hall International, Inc., *London*
Prentice-Hall of Australia, Pty., *Sydney*
Prentice-Hall of India Pvt. Ltd., *New Delhi*
Prentice-Hall of Japan, Inc., *Tokyo*
Prentice-Hall of Southeast Asia (Pte.) Ltd., *Singapore*
Editora Prentice-Hall do Brasil Ltda., *Rio de Janeiro*
Prentice-Hall Hispanoamericana, S.A., *Mexico*

Editor: William Booth
Design and Cover Illustration: Suzanne Boehler
Manufacturing Buyer: Lisa Kreuch

ISBN: 0-13-318809-4

Printed and bound in the U.S.A by
Arcata Graphics Book Group

1 2 3 4 5 AG 95 94 93 92 91

For Blake

CONTENTS

WHO GOES FISHING?

Judges. Criminals. Husbands. Wives. Children. Lovers. Bosses. Workers.

In my part of the country, in sight of Parliament Hill, workers fish so assiduously that the biggest newsprint mill in the world has to shut down at the opening of the trout season, because everybody has headed for the lakes and streams, just as the Eskimos drop everything when there are bears on the ice.

Our mill also has trouble with absenteeism in the deer season, the moose season and the duck season, but we are dealing here with fishing.

Doctors, lawyers, Indian chiefs all fish.

Our biggest corporations use fishing in client relations more than they use golf, and when the multinationals do it, they do it in Canadian waters.

Trade unions have their own camps on choice waters.

Politicians fish, and bureaucrats fish most of all.

Publishers fish with the paper companies.

Editors fish mostly on their own, and so do reporters.

Tinkers, tailors, barbers fish.

After the Gulf War, Barbara Bush took her George fishing—he is the fishingest United States president since Dwight Eisenhower, who spent as much time angling as he did golfing, the difference being that Eisenhower fished as a distinguished guest, whereas Bush plays host. Eisenhower got the fishing bug from Herbert Hoover, who said it was good for presidents, since "it is discipline in the equality of men, for all men are equal before fish."

They are not, of course, any more than women are. As in every sport involving coordination and craft, some are better than others, and I have known at least two anglers who could catch fish when all about them were being skunked, and do it with style and grace. I have known poachers who were merciless with fish, and then there are those pros on the TV shows, and the tournament fishermen with their frightening competence, giving no quarter. It's all part of fishing, and I hope to get the hang of it before I go into orbit.

Despite all this, in fifty-five years of writing, mostly about politics, when I wrote one piece a year about angling, editors complained, "You're always writing about fishing—get back to business!"

In vain do I plead that it's only one day a year and that a day spent fishing, or writing about it, is a day gained. Besides, more people clip from the fishing columns than the political ones, and if the fishing pieces stick in editors' craws so much, they must be more memorable than the others.

Or perhaps they fear the licence that applies to fish stories will spill over into political writing, where newspapers like to delude themselves that they are presenting facts. It has been my experience that most political stories make fish stories ring with the truth, by comparison.

Anyway, to hell with them—I keep writing occasionally about fishing, under the label of social commentary, since it is such an important part of so many lives.

Or, if it isn't, it should be, even though that would make the waters awfully crowded.

Better most should read about it; hence this book.

Perhaps it has something to do with going back to our roots.

Right back to the primeval ooze, I mean, because people have always fished, just as animals have, the ones that are properly equipped for the work with quick reflexes, handy paws and patience.

After all, most of us can't farm, as our ancestors did, even though our countries have more acreage under lawn grass than any other single crop, absorbing enormous amounts of our fresh water treasure and mixing it with more chemicals than we ever used in all the wars.

Besides, if we did farm, it wouldn't be worth our while, as witness the story of the farmer who was asked what he would do if he won a million in the lottery, and replied, "I guess I'd just keep on farming until it was gone."

(There is a story that, when Andy Warhol said everybody should be famous for fifteen minutes, it was a misprint. What he really said was "everybody should be farmers for fifteen minutes." That's about as long as most of us would last, unless we inherited the family agribusiness, which is probably owned by a multinational anyway, the way the cemetery business is.)

And we can't hunt, except for the ones in sporty garb or tractor hats who do it, not for the pot, but to keep blood-sports alive against a rising tide of public revulsion. The econuts may get to the anglers yet, because a barbed hook is not a pretty thing if you have it stuck in you. Anglers got a second-hand blow when the seal hunt in the Gulf of St. Lawrence was halted, permitting the seals to multiply and lay waste the salmon stocks, while filling the waters with defecation that put worms into the cod.

Few of us are as good at handicrafts as our forefathers, though there are some skilled hobbyists in our midst, operating on the same rule of self-subsidization as those who dabble in raising cattle.

But all can fish, whether monied or otherwise, though the monied anglers get the best crack at the best sport, and in some of their angling places it's like owning a yacht—if you have to ask the price, you can't afford it. In some circles, the price of Atlantic salmon taken on the fly is estimated at $1,000 a pound, not including the cost of getting it home. With aquaculture hitting its stride, that same fish, farm-born and raised, can be bought at the local market, fresh and cleaned, for as little as twenty-five bucks.

In Europe, ninety percent of the salmon eaten (and they eat a lot) is from fish farms—the Norwegians dominate the business the way they do North Sea oil or high-level cruising.

Agriculture is as old as humankind, while acquaculture is new, at least to the West. In China, they have been farming fish for centuries—I have seen them take three crops off a single piece of land—flood it for the rice, and after harvest fill it with fish, and, when the fish are fattened, drain it and put in a crop of kale, which thrives on the fish droppings.

In China, too, they fish for sport as well as the pot. When the People's Republic of China sent its first ambassador to Canada, he was treated with kid gloves by his diplomatic confrères and by the Canadian government, but I invited him up to the lake for some fishing. He was so grateful we became friends, and he got me a visa to visit his country, which was a journalistic coup at the time. On that visit, in Harbin, the hotel chef promised me a treat for dinner that night, and he brought it in under a silver cover, which he lifted with a flourish to reveal a large-mouth bass, beautifully grilled and more delicious than any I had eaten at home.

He had caught it himself, on rod and line, using techniques familiar the world over—one critic has called it the sport of fools, a bit of string with a worm on one end and an idiot on the other. I prefer to think of it as the blameless sport.

How far back does it go?

The first recorded fish stories are the ones in the Good Book, about the filling of the nets on Gallilee, and the one about the loaves and the fishes. We are never told what kind of fish materialized there on the mount to feed the multitude, and I bet they were large-mouth bass.

If one of today's game wardens had come along at that big feed, he would have arrested the whole bunch for going beyond their limit.

It happened once to a friend of mine in New Jersey, who was enjoying some of the "put-and-take" fishing that is all they have left on most of their streams. The tank truck from the hatchery comes along in the morning, puts in the fish, and by noon the anglers have caught them all, the limit per rod being six. The trick is to know what time the trucks are going to arrive, and what streams are being stocked on any given day, or at any given hour.

My friend had the right stream on this day, but the tank truck had not yet arrived. He was idly casting on the vacant waters when a truck drove by on the road behind him, and went over a bump with a big splash. He walked back to the road and found a dozen trout thrashing about on the wet pavement. As he was scooping them into his creel, along came the game warden and, despite his protestations, he was charged with having six fish over the limit, even though he hadn't hooked a single one. I have always counted that one of the most poignant of fish stories, especially since the warden impounded the fish as evidence.

The big thing is to know where they are.

Not suppose. Not hope. Not even pray!

You have to *KNOW* they're there.

Then you can fish, and exult in the scenery and the outdoors and the smells and the tastes of it, as long as you know the fish are there.

Catching them is another matter, involving skill, and luck, and weather, and season, time of day or night, the solunar tables, the Holy Bible, the Koran, the barometer, and such internal matters as hangovers, sunburn and whether a family of Merganser ducks has just spooked the pool and sent every fish into hiding.

But you won't fish in dead water, or if you do, you won't do it for long. The best way to know is if you have caught fish there before—and if you have, you never forget, however young you were when you did it, and however old you are now.

Another way is to know the reputation of the place, or to have heard first-hand, second-hand or third about anglers who have had luck there.

To have done it personally is best—to this day, I remember dark pools in brooks, some of them very small, that have yielded the pull of speckled trout and the joy of that prettiest of fish coming to hand, either for release or the creel.

Streams are best, but it is the same with lakes, big ones or small. Some have fish, some have none. You have to know. And dead lakes abound, as they always have—our grandfathers and their fathers knew places where there were no fish, and they shunned them, travelling long distances past many waters for the places they knew.

Sure, there are pleasures to be had from waters, besides fishing them. You can swim, you can sail, you can surf, you can paddle, paint, or rev a two-hundred-horsepower outboard so high the speedboat leaves scarcely any wake. You can watch loons and beaver, and marvel at the glories of the outdoors, but all these marvels will be enhanced if you think of the fish, and the sport to be had. The blameless sport, it has been called, by those who feel St. Peter doesn't deduct the days spent fishing from the allotted span.

Then there is the eating, and the giving of fish to neighbors and friends. The gift of a fish seems to mean something special, and it can heal rifts that seem set for life.

Our lake is famous for bass and pike, and the knowledge of this heightens the enjoyment of everything we do there, all year round. Even in winter, the ice fishermen come and bore their holes and rig their lines and sit there smoking, amid scenery that is more wonderful in winter than in summer, and a whole lot more peaceful. They may end the day empty-handed, but they know the fish are there, pike running up to twenty pounds, which stock the freezers of the rural folk and taste great when they are properly anointed and baked, served with the fiddleheads that abound in the Québec valleys, and are fatter, and at least as tasty, as the New Brunswick variety.

TO FLY, OR NOT TO FLY

S hort of using explosives, there is no bad way of fishing, though fly fishers will always maintain that tufts of feathers, hanks of hair, bits of tinsel and a hook constitute the best way.

The general rule of thumb worldwide is that the best way is the way that works.

I have seen fishermen on Chinese rivers, perched on punts no wider than racing shells, managing four cormorant ducks on strings, like so many acrobatic kites. For sheer dexterity of angler and line, this method tops them all, but it is not recommended for non-oriental fishers, especially if the fish being sought are too large to go into a cormorant's gullet.

Not all orientals fish in this spectacular manner—I knew a Canadian ambassador to Japan who once was invited to go fishing with some leading figures of the Japanese political and industrial community. On the appointed morning, two luxury buses pulled up at the palatial embassy residence, and the ambassador climbed aboard. Once he made himself comfortable in a plush armchair, he was plied with delicacies and drinks, and the party was quite merry when the buses pulled up at the lodge that was their destination. The ambassador had memorized the list of everybody who was making the trip, and all of them were on the first bus.

"Then who," he asked his host, "are the people on the second bus?"

"Why," came the surprised reply, "those are the girls!"

I never did get the rest of that fish story, but I don't think they used cormorants.

I have been in the highlands of Scotland in early spring, driving the narrow road to Tamantoul, which, in addition to whisky, is famous for its salmon fishing.

Since Scotland is where sport fishing for salmon is thought to have started, I trod softly and reverently on the holy ground, and found myself in a pub filled with anglers. Gentlemen anglers, that is, in one room, and their ghillies in another. I eased myself in with the ghillies and asked how the fishing was.

"Slow," came the reply. "Early yet."

On the walls of the pub were stuffed salmon of enormous length and girth—astonishing, since the streams thereabouts were so narrow. The plaque on one fish said it had weighed fifty-two pounds.

"What flies are doing best?" I asked.

"Flies?" came the reply. "We're not using flies. That's for later, after the natural hatch. There's no flies hereabouts yet."

"What are you using, then?"

"Worms, sir."

For the dedicated fly fisher, there was worse to come. Driving through the Scottish countryside, I noticed that most of the autos had racks on their roofs, the way Canadian cars do in ski country in winter.

Fastened to those racks, all rigged and ready for action, were spinning rods. No mistaking the hardware attached—lures that had never seen a feather or a hair. This was heavy artillery, and it was for salmon fishing, as I saw when drivers would leap out, grab the rod and start casting.

The only place I saw a fly rod was on the River Dee, where some fifty anglers were wading a long pool in which the salmon were jumping. They were fishing it the way Britons do so many things, by queuing. An angler would enter the top of the pool, take a cast, and move three steps down. Another angler would follow, each taking three steps after every cast, until the line extended to the foot of the pool, where the first angler would clamber onto the bank and walk back to the top of the pool, repeating the process. I watched for two hours and counted at least two dozen jumping fish, some of them rising within arm's length of their pursuers. Nobody caught anything, but I was told that, if anybody had, the others would have reeled in to make room for the contest, which is more than sports do for one another in crowded pools on rivers in Ontario or Nova Scotia, or the St. John in New Brunswick.

My view of sportsmanship in Scotland was softened somewhat by an experience of my friend Jack Sanderson, a man I always admired because, while he worked for bankers, he always said he preferred to fish with journalists. It wasn't that we fished better than bankers, but that we told better stories around the dinner table.

Sanderson was a handsome man, who would have made a wonderful duke in, say, the eighteenth century. He once wangled an invitation to fish a private section of the Dee near Balmoral Castle and, after a few hours of wading in the rain, he sighted a fellow angler downstream of him, and worked his way toward this figure, in the process losing track of the boundary, and crossing into forbidden territory.

He realized his mistake and called out an apology to the other angler, whereupon he was given a signal to keep coming.

"It's quite all right," said the fisher, casting expertly the while. "They don't usually take in the rain, and a bit of company is welcome."

Beneath the rain hood, Sanderson recognized what was probably the most familiar face in Britain, and he thanked Her Majesty and fished contentedly beside the Queen Mother for half an hour, before saying his farewells with a bow. She was not, he assured me, using a spinning rod—she showed him her fly box and offered to lend him a fly, but he stuck with what he had.

The most famous salmon fishing in the world, I suppose, is on Canada's west coast, but it has nothing to do with fly fishing, and is more a matter of dredging in salt water, at least in my experience. Flies are used in some streams for the steelhead, and one of the world's most expert fly fishers, Roderick Haig-Brown, pursued the sport assiduously, chronicling his adventures in some of the best fishing literature ever penned.

But, for the everyday west coast fishermen, the technique is trolling, and a dull business it can be in the cockpit of a motor cruiser, rods resting in holders, and some two hundred other boats keeping pace, all the anglers sitting idly by, waiting for a bite. When the action comes, it can be hot and heavy, but I have never been there, though I have seen the charter boats returning to the marina at Vancouver's Bayshore Inn with heavy catches.

The downriggers and weights that are used to get the baits to the proper depth are so heavy that they slow the boat, the saving grace being that they have ingenious devices that unsnap the hardware when a fish is on, giving the salmon a

relatively free play. In all cases, the object is to boat the fish as quickly as possible.

The best fishing I have ever had in western waters was in the company of Mike Cramond, longtime fish and game editor of *The Vancouver Province* and John Diefenbaker's favorite fishing companion.

Mike took me "mooching" at Squamish, since I had expressed a preference for light tackle and a distaste for trolling. The fly rods he brought along would have been right at home on the Miramichi, even though we were fishing in salt water that could be ruinous to the rods and reels. Mike said not to worry, as long as we washed everything thoroughly at day's end.

The prospects did not seem propitious, because there were fifty boats drifting around the bay, everybody mooching for Spring salmon, the western species that most resembles Salmo Salar, the Atlantic salmon and King of Fish. (They have a west coast salmon called the King, but we won't talk about that.)

Mike showed me the technique. Tiny herring for bait, a light weight on the line, and let it down deep—at least fifty feet, and then sit there. We didn't sit long. I had one, and let out a yelp, and Mike said to reel in like crazy. I cranked as fast as I could, and said I must have lost the fish, because the line was slack.

"Reel!" roared Mike.

Reel I did, until my cranking hand was numb. Then, suddenly, the fish broke the surface, and jumped. I kept cranking until the line went tight.

"Now," said Mike, "play him!" There were cheers from neighboring boats as that salmon cavorted around, using tricks I thought only his distant eastern brethren knew.

The fish was landed, my hook was baited, and down it went again, connecting with another Spring almost immediately.

Another mad bout of cranking, another splash, another fight, another fish on board.

Those two salmon were the only ones taken in the entire flotilla that day, and I had to agree with Diefenbaker that Cramond was a guide beyond compare.

"Just plain luck," said he. "Just wanted to show you how we use light tackle out here."

He had the bright idea that we should send one of the salmon back to John Diefenbaker in Ottawa, so we arranged to

have it packed and shipped by air express to my Southam colleague, Charles King, with instructions to take it to Dief the
Chief.

For King, it would be a peace offering, because Diefenbaker
had not spoken to him, or recognized his existence, since King
had written a story about a Diefenbaker visit to the Yukon, in
the course of which he had caught one fish. King, toting up the
total cost of Diefenbaker's trip, dubbed it "the $10,000 fish,"
and Dief's rage knew no bounds.

But when King showed up at Diefenbaker's doorstep with
our fresh Spring salmon, the old grudge was forgotten and
they remained friends to the day of his death. It bore out the
theory that, if you want to cement a friendship, or repair one,
bring an offering of a fish—one fish if it's a salmon, several if
it's trout. It may not always work, but it's a better bet than
candy or liquor. Lawrence Freiman, the merchant prince of
Ottawa, usually referred to me warmly as "my country neighbor who brings me trout."

I didn't tell him that only some of them were caught on
the fly.

By that time, the places I fished for trout were mostly spinning spots, and we kidded ourselves that the lures we used were like flies, really—tiny Mepps and EGBs that we changed according to the time of day and the weather. We always carried fly rods in the rowboat, but only the purest of purists unlimbered them, and then only for a few token casts before turning to the hardware.

I once fished with a distinguished general of the Canadian Army, who brought with him a piece of wooden shingle he had carved into the shape of a minnow, the underside equipped with two triple gang hooks. I eyed the thing uneasily, while he slapped a line on it and threw it over the side with a splash, saying he always kept it in the water just for luck.

We proceeded to rig our rods but, before we could make a cast, there was the most ungodly splash, and spray was flying all around. The general grabbed the line on his wooden minnow and horsed aboard the best trout of the trip, measuring twenty-three inches, and fat—a very pretty fish, betrayed by a most unsporting lure. No apology was offered, but we were skunked for the rest of the day, and I think it was divine intervention, though it may have been my stubborn insistence that we give fly fishing a really good chance, as in olden times. Other parties did better that day, but I suspect they were using worms.

THE BEST SPECKLED TROUT FISHING IN THE WORLD

The year the birch trees died in Québec the hills were like cemeteries. Dead birch trees like sentinels in every direction, lining the valleys, ringing the lakes, outlining the contours of the land like a million strokes of chalk.

Nobody knew why the birches died, and this was before the recognition of pollution, so nobody blamed anybody else. There was an acceptance of the phenomenon as something that happened every so often in nature's cycle, and there was confidence the birches would come back, as indeed they have since the big dieback.

Indian lore failed to inform us on possible past tragedies of this sort, though the loss of all the birch trees must have been a serious matter, in a society that relied on this most remarkable of hardwoods for everything from shelter and warmth to transportation.

The loss of the birch trees didn't hurt the fishing in the parts of Québec that were stricken, and once you got used to all those gleaming silver stumps you could even imagine they had a beauty of their own, and you would not miss the distinctive light green of the birches that heralded the first of the spring fishing, or the brilliant yellows they painted as a backdrop for the brief fall days of fishing for trout, the mid-September close of season having robbed anglers of the full burst of autumn color against which to pursue the trout, whose speckles and deep red hues were such a match for the glories of the leaves. That early green of the birches in May had always been the signal that the ice was out and that the trout would be waiting in the clear, cold waters, and there were those who said the first week of fishing was always the best. In more leisurely times, anglers looked forward to the first three weeks, and they called it "going to camp."

It was in sight of those legions of dead birch trunks, their branches groping out and upward like arms clutching for the sky, that we enjoyed the last of the great speckled trout fishing in North America, the quest for the wild trout of Québec.

If that fishing is as good today as it was thirty years ago, it is a tribute to successive Québec governments which, amid all the preoccupations of sovereignty and assertion of the French Fact, found time also to safeguard a resource as old as the land itself—and these were said to be the oldest hills and lakes in the Western Hemisphere.

The earliest explorer chronicles tell of the trout, and the natives knew about them ages before that. The salmon were another matter altogether, and we will get to them later, as befits anglers who, if they come to fishing salmon first, will never be satisfied fishing anything else. The salmon come last—not late in life, but after a full taste has been had of trout fishing, with bass and pike and pickerel thrown in for variety and to measure the beauty of the speckles. When we get to the salmon we will speak of little else, and there will be room for that.

It was the separatist government of René Lévesque that cancelled the leases of the fishing clubs, under whose auspices the trout fishing had been preserved for a hundred years. The trout, for all its fighting qualities, cannot stand up to unrestrained angling pressure the way bass and pike can, and even heavy poaching of "private" waters can finish the fly fishing, especially when the poachers introduce the minnows of the sunfish, perch and suckers, which can put a trout lake out of business forever and turn it into something else, abounding with what the angler calls trash fish.

(There are salmon rivers where trout themselves are called trash fish, because sports are after larger game and voracious trout can tear flies to pieces, especially dry flies, which they drown beyond redemption. As a trout lover, I could never stand to hear them called trash and insisted on putting them back, even though they are known to devour the salmon parr and fry, even more destructively than the hated Merganser fish ducks do. And a lunch of fresh-caught trout by the banks of a salmon stream is as memorable as any part of the outing, except the fight itself.)

After the cancellation of the leases, it was widely predicted that the best trout fishing anywhere would be ruined, but it was not to be—the separatists knew more about conservation than pessimists had thought they would. The regulations they brought in had no parallel in any other Canadian or American jurisdiction, and by enforcing them, they not only saved the trout, they enhanced them—and today the best trout waters are as good as they ever were, or maybe even better. This, of course, involves an element of conjecture, because old logbooks tell of fly fishing so productive it must have been monotonous, with a catch on every cast, and sometimes two or three fish on a single throw.

We had such fishing the year the birches died, and I can remember almost every detail of a Laurentide Park lake that had been closed to fishing for four years, and was opened in time for our party to get first crack at it. There were twenty of us fishing, including the prince of Canadian anglers, Greg Clark, and the rajah of Québec game writers, George Carpenter, and both said they had never seen anything like it. The Québec government was represented by Philippe Gagnon, who cast a fly with almost loving tenderness, and took us to the right places as though shepherding pilgrims to Lourdes.

Country folk have a better crack at the first fishing than city people do, and there has always been a tradition that early-season poaching by rural residents is the exercise of an ancient rite, rather than a breach of law.

... AND THE WORST

One of the biggest scams ever pulled on tourists in the Maritime provinces (apart from the Magnetic Hill, which is a trick, and the Tidal Bore, which is at least honestly boring) is the notion that a visitor can catch speckled trout merely by wetting a line in any lake or stream.

There may have been tourists who caught trout in the Maritimes, summer tourists I mean, but I have never been in their company nor, indeed, have I heard of them. The best book ever written about trout fishing has a Nova Scotia locale, set in what is now Kejimkujik National Park. It is by Ernest Thomson Seton and it is called *The*

Tent Dwellers. It was written at the turn of the century and re-issued twenty years ago by Abercombie & Fitch, in their terminal New York delirium. The New Yorkers of that story have wild and wonderful adventures with the trout in the Nova Scotia wilds, but to get there they had to travel by steamer, train and buckboard, followed by long canoe paddles, and their reward was trout fishing to the point of exhaustion.

But that was long ago, and things are different now. I had an uncle-in-law named Bert Seeton (no relation to the author), who was chief Nova Scotia agent for the Great West Life Insurance Company—at least, that is what he said he was. Uncle Bert was thoroughly schooled in the Maritime art of genteel poverty—keeping up the appearances of wealth while having none—and his real avocation was fishing. Living in Nova Scotia is a lot different from touring there, and the natives know where the fish are, and at what time of year they bite. In the case of the speckled trout, it is a week after the ice goes out, or ten days at the most—a time of year when there are few tourists on the road.

Uncle Bert made his rounds of the province with his fishing tackle in the car—trout for spring and fall, salmon for summer—and it was never clear when he had any time to sell insurance. He must have sold some, though, because the Great West Life invited him to join their head-office staff in Winnipeg, and the trip there was the longest time he was ever out of Nova Scotia. He got off the train in Winnipeg in the morning, and got back on the train for the east that afternoon, having inquired after the speckled trout and the Atlantic salmon, and finding he had left all that behind.

Uncle Bert once told me he had caught 2,500 salmon and 15,000 speckled trout, and that was after he quit and promised to leave me his rods. He never did—his housekeeper got them, I think—but he did give me his copy of *The Tent Dwellers*, which has provided so much pleasure through the years. He never did show me where the trout fishing was, because I was from outside the province, but he did talk about his favorite salmon river, Moser's, near Ecum Secum on the Eastern Shore. Most of his life he had that river to himself, and you can go there now to wet a line, if you don't mind fishing elbow-to-elbow with fellow anglers.

I have done a lot of holidaying in Nova Scotia, and a lot of angling, but I have never caught a speckled trout there, even though the tourist literature was festooned with them. I assume all those photographs were taken the week after the ice went out, and that the grinning anglers were natives who had taken their fur coats off just long enough to have their pictures taken.

In line with the doctrine that you have to suffer to get to the good fishing, I once spent the hardest day of my life in company with local journalist and guide Eric Dennis, the smart member of the Halifax newspaper family, who promised that, if we could hike over an escarpment to a hidden lake, we would catch trout. I discovered later that the true name of that height of land was Heartbreak Ridge, and I spare the reader the details, except to say that we had to drag a wooden punt with us as we went, thus laying waste our powers before we ever go to the lake. In the end, it wasn't worth our time—there was not a trout to be had, nor any fish of any kind, apart from the Connors Bros. sardines we had brought with us.

Not long after this adventure, I was making a speech to a tourist promotion dinner in Halifax, and seized the occasion to denounce the tourist literature's use of speckled trout as a lure. There was, I said, not a trout in the province from the opening of the tourist season to its close, no matter how good the fishing might be in May.

This so roused the ire of my hosts that I was denounced by the chairman of the dinner, who drew applause when he said he would speak to me after, in the hope there might yet be time for me to change my sinful ways. Speak to me, he did, and not only that, he promised to arrange some fishing for me that very week that would change my views. He would put me in touch with the best fishing guide in Nova Scotia, and we would catch trout enough to sink the boat.

Done.

I dropped all plans to return to the outside world and put myself at the disposal of the Nova Scotia government, whose instructions were to present myself at a certain farmhouse back of New Germany, which itself is back of Bridgewater, and there I would find the best damn guide in the whole province. The rest would revise my opinion of Nova Scotia trout fishing.

I found the farm, introduced myself to the guide, and we set out towards his favorite lake, I having declared my doubts about the existence of trout, and he expressing confidence that my views would be changed.

We got to the lake, boarded the boat and cast off. There followed three hours of assiduous angling, with fly, spinner and trolling lures, with no result. My guide unlimbered, from under the thwarts of the boat, an assemblage of spinners, lenses, whistles and bells that was half as long as the boat and would have frightened an alligator. Without a word he tied it on, and we went up and down the lake, my rod groaning under the strain.

No luck.

We went back to the farmhouse for lunch, and the lady of the house had prepared a mountain of chicken and potatoes, topped off by a raspberry pie the like of which I had seldom seen or smelled, let alone eaten. I was into my second piece of pie when the son of the family, unimpressed by my ravings about the greatness of the pie, allowed as how it was nothing compared to "that restaurant pie in Bridgewater."

Turned out he was talking about raisin pie, the Nova Scotia restaurant variety of which was as thick as an asphalt shingle, and roughly the same texture.

I did not stay to argue, because the guide had promised that since the trout fishing was a washout, we should try for the salmon in the Mersey River. I objected that I had no proper gear, and he said that would be no problem, leading me to a back shed where he had an assemblage of hooks and weights and heavy line that made the place look more like an arsenal than a tackle room.

Like most city anglers, I had always assumed that most country people were poachers at heart, since they were inclined to regard all local waters and their contents as theirs by right, the fish to be taken by whatever means worked best, by day or, mostly, by night.

It had not occurred to me that the Nova Scotia government had referred me to a poacher, but there it was—he showed me a series of fearsome-looking jigs, consisting of hunks of lead with big cod hooks imbedded in them. These, he said, would be our tackle for the afternoon's fishing—you threw them over the backs of the basking salmon in the pool and gave a pluck, whereupon the jig imbeded itself in the fish and you horsed it to shore. It would be important to have a cigarette going, so you could touch it to the monofilament line should a warden chance by, thus severing the line and leaving the salmon to swim off with the evidence.

I should have called the police at this stage of the game. I must have been in some kind of a trance, perhaps caused by the romance of it all—here I was in the inner sanctum of rural poacherdom, a veritable Jamaica Inn of the poaching game, and we were setting out for the river. Away we went, in my car, the guide having said it would be less recognizable than this. I realized what he meant, the moment we turned off the main road to approach the river—the guide uttered an oath and, looking in the rear-view mirror, I could see another car up our tail. "Skunk!" said the guide. It was the warden—my car might have been strange to the neighborhood, but my companion was not, and the warden recognized him and fastened onto us like a leech.

The guide said it wouldn't be worth getting out of the car, and there probably weren't any salmon in the pool, anyway. But this was the closest I had been to the Mersey, so I insisted on getting out, and the two of us stood on the bank, looking into the pond, where indeed about seven salmon were assembled, barely twitching to hold their own against the current. The warden got out of his car and approached us, and I introduced myself, while my guide kept his silence.

"You plannin' to fish any?" the warden asked me.

"Nope, just sightseeing," said I.

"You bring any tackle?"

"No," I answered, truthfully. By no stretch of the imagination could what was in my trunk be called tackle, except perhaps in the sense of block and tackle, as used in heavy construction.

"You must have a lot of river to cover," I observed.

"Not if I know where to look," said he, settling himself on a nearby rock.

Obviously, we were at an impasse, and might as well move on. We got into the car and backed out, and the warden was right after us. Clearly, we were not going to get out of his sight, which was a good thing for the salmon in the river, and a good thing for my conscience and possibly my criminal record.

We got back to the farmhouse and I bade my guide farewell, resolved that, when I made my next report on Nova Scotia trout fishing, it would be stronger than anything I had said at that dinner.

Later that summer, I made my peace with fishing in Nova Scotia, thanks to my friend Eric Dennis, who must have had an attack of conscience for what he had put me through on Heartbreak Ridge.

He suggested we try some fly fishing in Hubbard's Cove, on whose shores he had his summer cottage. He had never tried it, but he heard there was a run of tinker mackerel in the cove and that they might just be inclined to take a fly.

Each of us had leaders rigged for three flies—the kind you used to be able to buy ready-made, before multiple fly casting came to be frowned upon by the conservationists. We took our trout rods and went forth on the waters of the cove, and there ensued two hours of the busiest fishing either of us had ever experienced, consisting, as it did, of three fish on every cast. Lovelies they were, too—the mackerel running just above pan-sized, and the occasional pollock a bit bigger. We uttered roars of excitement while we pulled them in, until our arms ached and our voices grew hoarse. All of this took place on one of the smallest and most heavily-settled coves on the South Shore of Nova Scotia, amid yachts and fishing boats, which were moored all around, and within smelling distance of the fish plant that was the main industry of the village.

When we had had enough, we turned to shore and put our catch on a stringer that it took the two of us to lift. We had our pictures taken, and proceeded to distribute the mackerel through the village—welcome gifts, because there is nothing tastier than a mackerel fresh from the sea—not even a steak from its big relative, the horse mackerel, or tuna; the ones the fishermen brought to the fish plant and chopped up with axes, sending the meat off to New York and Japan.

I reported back to the people at the Nova Scotia tourist bureau, telling them that the best guide in Nova Scotia had been unable to deliver, and that my views on trout fishing were unaltered. I didn't bother turning him in for his perfidy, since it was clear the local warden had him in his sights, and he would be unable to put those jigs to their improper use. At least, that's what I told my conscience—no doubt, in the dark of night, by the glow of a cigarette, that man would have his salmon to go with the raspberry pie.

At any rate, I had a positive suggestion to give the tourist bureau. Stop advertising trout fishing for all, and put the emphasis on fly fishing in the coves. Nova Scotia has more coves than any other seagirt place on earth, and it has long been a smugglers' paradise, whether the stuff being smuggled was rum or dope. Turn the fishermen lose with their fly rods, and everybody will go home happy.

Whether or not his advice was taken, I do not know. Fishing parties are taken into the inshore waters, and they dangle lines off pieces of wood and occasionally bring something in, but there is little sport in it and you couldn't call it angling, unless you were like the fisherman who was handlining off Halifax Harbor, and hooked into a giant tuna that proceeded to tow his dory up and down the harbor, being brought to boat only after a tussle of six hours. The fisherman towed his trophy to shore, where it was found to weigh over a thousand pounds, and he put in for the world's record for tuna caught by hand. Turned out, though, that the record keepers only recognized trophy fish caught on rods and, since the fisherman's stick was only a foot long, he didn't qualify. If he'd had a rod in the boat, he could have tied one on and lied about it, but he didn't.

I can imagine how his arms must have ached, and it reminded me of why my father said he would never go deep-sea fishing for tuna, which was quite the sport off Nova Scotia at the time—they even had world tournaments, with big-time news coverage, until the fish went somewhere else. Prince Edward Island, New Brunswick and Newfoundland all tried to get in on the tuna act while the fish were running, and they all hung pictures of tuna on their tourist literature, as long as a single fish bothered to show up. Newfoundland produced one of the best fishing films ever, *A Double In Tuna*, as a result of a cameraman being on board the day they hooked into two tuna at the same time. Heaven knows how many fishermen were lured to Newfoundland by that one, but not Father.

What he said was that fighting and landing a horse mackerel was like bucksawing two cords of wood, and nothing on earth would persuade him to do that. It was Father who took the sport out of spincasting by likening the spinning reel to a wall can-opener, and saying that a day of spinning was the equivalent of opening five hundred cans of beans, something he would not go out of his way to do. If it wasn't fly fishing, he said, it wasn't fishing at all—and being a native New Brunswicker, he knew where they were.

THE HORWOOD BOIL

There are no poor fishing days, though there are plenty of days of poor fishing. The point is to fish when you can, and the good days will come—you can't catch anything if your line isn't in the water, and if you aren't fishing you won't be there for the flurry, if it hits.

Every day on the water is better than most days off it, and the memories glow warm in the mind. But the really good days remain as vivid as when they happened, fish by fish and cast by cast, the places etched to the last detail of shore, tree or rock.

These are just the good days—my father and his father had to search for good fishing in isolated lakes in New Brunswick, and often came home empty. There were barren lakes and streams then, as now—nobody knows how many Canadian lakes have never held fish, but the number is high. Yes, there were good old days, and there are good days if you get lucky.

Here are some of mine, starting with the Horwood Boil.

The Magannassippi River has as many spellings as there are letters in its name, all of them phonetic renderings of the Indian word, and most of them sanctified on maps of Western Québec, depending on the dates. It's reminiscent of T.E. Lawrence's comeback to an editor, who had chided him for spelling the name of an Arabian camel twelve different ways in the manuscript for *The Seven Pillars of Wisdom*. He responded with three additional versions, adding, "She was a splendid beast."

The Magannassippi was, and is, a splendid river, draining magnificent stands of timber and yielding, it is said, good bass fishing in midsummer. But it is not the bass that have lured anglers into that wilderness country for more than a century and a half; it is the trout that abound in the vast system of lakes that drains into the river and then into the mighty Ottawa.

The most accessible of these lakes had long been under lease to the Magannissippi Fish and Game Club, started by Ottawa River lumber barons in the late nineteenth century, and eventually expanded to include an impressive list of United States sportsmen, who would come to each spring and fall camp for stays of two or three weeks. Canadian generals, admirals and Supreme Court judges were members or frequent guests, and bosses sometimes brought favored employees in for weekend treats, if there was a vacant bed.

Thus it was that Robert Southam, publisher of *The Ottawa Citizen* and a long-time member, invited me to join him for some fishing and, though I didn't know it at the time, to be looked over as a prospective member, since I had a Québec address and they were looking to bolster their Québec content, in hopes of preserving their lease. Having recently suffered the loss of the Denholm Angling Club through lease cancellation, I was delighted at the chance of some trout fishing, and away we went up the Trans-Canada Highway, beyond Deep River and Chalk River to Deux Rivières, across on a lumber company ferry and into the woods.

Introductions all round at the bustling main camp, a splendid structure of logs and screened varandahs, with a huge dining room. A full complement of members was there, and I remember most vividly Mr. Fritz Krebs of Cleveland, Ohio, an industrialist and sportsman of the old Teddy Roosevelt school of American outdoorsmen, a breed not yet extinct. Krebs wore pince-nez spectacles and high collars, britches and leggings, and he spoke with courtesy to the newcomer, apologizing for the fishing not being very promising. Others explained that Mr. Krebs (they all called him that) was not fishing himself that week—he was busy trapping trout fingerlings in a lake where they abounded, and carrying them in pails to other lakes where the fishing was off. That a man would come for two weeks from Cleveland to absorb himself in such a project did not seem to surprise the other members, but it certainly impressed me!

When it came time for the fishing spots to be apportioned for the weekend, our party of two drew Horwood Lake. This brought a shrug from my host, which I took to mean we might have had better luck. It was later that evening that Mr. Southam told me about Horwood, and the legend of the Boil. He had never seen it himself, he said, but other members swore they had—the surface of the lake foaming with frantic fish. It was his hope to see the phenomenon one day, because otherwise the fishing was indifferent at Horwood, though the birdwatching was good.

The ritual of well-to-do club fishermen on the trail is precise, orchestrated by the staff at camp when everything is packed in the morning—the key item being the billy can, for preparing soup and tea at the lunch site. The tea ritual is as elaborate as anything known to the Japanese, and any suggestion that insulated containers would be more convenient is dismissed, since it would eliminate the business of preparing the fire, rigging a stick to hold the can, and the illusion of roughing it on trails that have been described as wall-to wall pine needles.

On our Horwood expedition, we parked the vehicle on the shoulder of the gravel road, lathered ourselves up with fly dope, shouldered our packs, picked up the rods and headed into the bush. It was a short trail—a few hundred meters to a rustic dock from which we could see the expanse of the lake.

There was no breeze, and hardly a sound except for the buzz of the flies around our heads. Host Southam produced his key and unlocked the chain that bound the boat to the dock, signalling me to take my place in the stern, for starters—he would row, and would let me know when it was my turn "in the engine room," as he called it. I got my rod ready, tied on a fly and started casting.

Nobody knows how many casts a fisherman makes in the course of a day. Certainly, enough that if the same amount of energy were expended in some other activity, say scrubbing floors or painting a fence, there would be complaints. On this day, the work was unproductive, and we fished out the morning with no result, my host having signalled after the first hour that it was permissible to switch to the spinning gear and the hardware. Since the ritual was the same at my old club, this caused me no problem—by the time that club folded, fly fishing was but a dream, and we were using worms.

Mr. Southam is a man of few words, which, on the whole, is no bad thing in a fishing companion, some of my happiest days having been spent in boats with friends who scarcely uttered a word, apart from "let's move," or "your turn," or "sorry," when they would snag you. Other gems of conversation would be "let's eat," or "let's go," or the more stimulating "got one!"

Few words ruffled the quiet of Horwood this day, and when we landed for lunch, my host did his rustic bit with the fire and the billy can, complaining only that some of the wood I brought was damp. He brightened when I produced a flask filled with sherry, and dumped it into the boiling consommé, a trick he had not encountered before and one that he felt might brighten my chances of acceptance by the membership. We lunched in silence, he made the tea and, after tending to our ablutions, we set off to fish out the afternoon, Mr. Southam saying he would be paying more attention to the birds than to the fishing, his binoculars at the ready.

Up to mid-afternoon, we had three smallish trout to show for our efforts and, while this was all right with me, I had to wonder about the mystique of the Magannassippi Club, long reputed as the last outpost of really great speckled trout fishing in Western Québec. These, after all, were sacred, protected waters, far from the pollution and the poaching that had cut into the speckled trout fishing in more accessible haunts. I was toying with these thoughts and flogging away with my spinner, when there came a rustling sound, not so much of leaves being stirred as of a stirring in the water. Mr. Southam dropped the oars and leapt to his feet—rocking the boat considerably as he did so. He looked in the direction of the disturbance and muttered something that I took to be "Holy Jeez!" Since he was not given to profanity, at least not in the presence of his employees, I realized something of significance was afoot.

"The Boil!" he said, in what, for him, was a shout.

"What Boil?" I inquired.

"The Boil, you silly bastard. The Horwood Boil!"

I looked where he was pointing, and, sure enough, there was a roiling of the water, with flecks of foam flying, and fish jumping.

It was coming our way.

"Put away that goddam spinner and tie on Tec's Fancy," Southam commanded.

"What in hell is Tec's Fancy?" asked I.

"Tec Morphy's fly for the Horwood Boil!" barked Southam. "Everybody has one."

"Never heard of it," I said.

"Oh, God," said Mr. Southam, tying a huge yellow fly to his line. "I've only got one—never used it in my life. Have you got a Mickey Finn?"

That I had, obtained from its inventor, Greg Clark, and long kept idle in my flybox, because it looked too big and bright to ever tempt a trout. Do trout eat bumble bees?

"Tie it on," said Mr. Southam. "They're coming right past us, and they're coming fast."

They sure were. Within about thirty seconds they were within reach, and each one of us had one on. Both fish fought fiercely, and it took us half a minute to land them.

"Faster, faster," said Mr. Southam. "Get them while they're hot!"

Both of us were standing up, working feverishly. Every cast, a fish. Same fly—him with Tec's Fancy, me with Mickey Finn.

"The Boil!" he kept shouting. "The real, honest-to-God, Horwood Boil!"

I felt something snap, but paid no heed—just kept fishing, as ordered.

It lasted for all of ten minutes, and then everything went quiet.

The Boil didn't pass beyond us, it just ended, as quickly as it began. There was still the foam from all the commotion, but the trout were no longer there.

Mr. Southam turned and looked at me, sweat dripping, and he started to laugh.

"You silly bugger," he said, pointing. "What the hell are you doing with your pants down?"

I looked below, and they were.

In the action, my suspenders had snapped, and my pants were down below my knees. I had fished the Horwood Boil in my underwear.

"Geez," said Mr. Southam, "I don't know what the members would say if they saw this. It certainly violates the dress code of the club."

I thought of Fritz Krebs, and had to agree I was a long way from the gentleman-sportsman image. Pulling up my pants, I mumbled an apology. Mr. Southam said he would give me the address of his outfitter, so I could get stronger stuff.

When I had made myself tidy, we agreed to call it a day and return to camp, Mr. Southam saying he now felt his life as a fisherman was complete. He had fished the Horwood Boil.

"You haven't got another slug of that sherry, have you?" he asked. As it happened, I had. We sipped in silence, and the birds sang all around.

THE SELF-
ADMINISTERED
PRIEST

There was a fuss at the fall camp
when one of the American
members arrived with his dog,
a big black Labrador.

There was nothing in the club
regulations about dogs, but
nobody had ever brought one
before, and this member insisted on bringing the dog into the
clubhouse and having it sleep
beside his bed in the dormitory.
Other members grieved, and a
spirited debate ensued, occupy-
ing most of the first night in camp
and putting tempers on edge.

I have always been of a doggy
disposition myself, and have the
same feeling about dogs in camp that I
have about women—they add to, rather

than detract from, any gathering, provided they are not overly hostile or overly affectionate, both of which tendencies can have an offputting effect on others present.

I remember interviewing Ms Katie Cooke when she was Canada's first commissioner of women, and asking her how she felt about that great Canadian stag event, the fishing trip. She gave me a quick comeback! "I have no objection to men on fishing trips, as long as they don't get in my way when I'm casting."

But we are dealing with dogs here, and in particular, this big black Lab that had been introduced into our midst and was taking up a prominent place in front of the fire, as dogs are wont to do. A better-behaved dog it would be hard to imagine, but it was on principle that other members were objecting to his presence, and the owner of the dog was taking it badly, and putting up a spirited fight against the proposition that the dog be banished to an outbuilding and forbidden clubhouse privileges for the full two weeks of the offending member's stay.

There was a split in the thirty or so members present, with the majority favoring keeping the dog out, and this was the final ruling, but not before I had made a strong pitch for letting the dog in. What decided the matter was the old argument about what would happen if everybody brought a dog and thay all had the run of the place, which would lead to God knew what commotion inside the precincts, and might even open the possibility of, well, women. Wives, even.

The argument was lost, and the secretary was delegated to run off an addition to the camp rules about dogs—members being discouraged from bringing them, and it being clearly understood that they were to be housed in outbuildings if brought, and prevented from barking within earshot of the clubhouse.

I thought no more of the incident until several days later, when the luck of the day's fishing draw brought my companions and me the right to fish three of the best lakes on the lease—Percival, Bowie and Forgie. There were three in our party—Bob Southam, Dick White and me, and we prepared to set out with anticipation after breakfast, Mr. Southam being the designated driver of the club's oldest and most disreputable Jeep. It seems to be a rule of fishing that the swankier the club, the worse the vehicles, and each member had his own sense of inverted pride about being able to master machines with wonky transmissions and brakes that had shot their best in the Second World War.

Mr. Southam and Mr. White were old naval buddies from that conflict, so I left it to them to stow the gear, including some patented rod holders, which White had devised to ensure the rods safe passage over some of the foulest roads in the universe.

I was watching the packing operation, when the American with the dog sidled up to me and said he understood we were going to Percival. I said we were, and he said he had fished it the day previous and had discovered something quite remarkable, by accident. The far end of the lake was covered with lily pads. He had flicked a cast into them, just to see if he could hit a tiny piece of open water, and *whammo!* A trout took the fly. And every time he cast into the lily pads, the same thing happened. The spot was stiff with them, he whispered, adding he was grateful for the fight I had put up in support of his dog.

I thanked him, and joined Messrs. Southam and White for the drive in to Percival.

Drive is too good a word for it. It was more like a thrash, every rock and root being transmitted into the posteriors of the passengers, especially if you were in the back seat, as I was, with its remembrance of World War II that the back seat of a Jeep must be the most uncomfortable place to be in any vehicle, except for being underneath. When we came to the final descent to the landing at Percival, it was clear that Mr. Southam had lost control, since he was pumping the brake pedal without any perceivable effect on the speed of the vehicle. Downward we flew, and the waters of the lake rose to meet us, or so it seemed. I expected an order from the driver to jump for our lives, but at a critical moment he gave the steering wheel a spin and, amazingly, it seemed still to be connected to the wheels. The Jeep slewed around and slammed into a tree, amid a cloud of dust, and cries of anguish from me.

"Made it," said Mr. Southam.

"Well done, old boy," said Mr. White.

"You always stop that way?" I inquired.

"Always," said Mr. Southam. "What do you think those marks are on the tree? Anybody hurt?"

Only my dignity, I thought, extricating myself from the wreck and sorting out my gear. The rods, sure enough, had remained secure in the patented holders, and nothing was busted.

We unlocked the boat and climbed aboard, with me delegated to do the rowing, as the newest member. We made a couple of circuits of the lake without much action, and finally it was proposed that we tie up at the far end and take the portage though to Bowie, the next lake. From there we would go to Forgie, at the top of the trail, and the lake most favored by the membership, year in and year out, as a producer.

I decided to conceal the information given me by our American colleague, knowing that we would be coming back this way later in the day, after fishing the two upper lakes. And anyway, the lily pads didn't look all that tempting—they were so tightly bunched there was hardly a spot between them where you could drop a fly.

So we tied up the boat and hit the trail for Bowie, fighting our way across it without a bite, and deciding to go right ahead on up to Forgie. The trail is one of the steepest in the whole club layout—so arduous that, in earlier times, members had been known to climb up to Forgie and stay there for a week or more in a log cabin that was built there for the purpose.

The trudge up the Forgie portage takes about thirty minutes at what I call my best pace. Indeed, it is my only pace—something I settle into in the first ten steps, and I don't think it would be much faster if a bear was after me, or much slower if the trail was knee-deep in gravel. It is a slow lope, and it even gets into my brain in the form of a rhythm, the sort of thing I imagine Fred Astaire might have heard during one of his numbers, only he did it faster. The big hazard for me on the trail has always been the intrusion of a TV singing commercial, which, once it gets started, I can't get rid of, sometimes for days. There is one from radio that still lurks in the back of my mind, waiting to be let out, and when it gets the upper hand it just goes around and around like an endless tape, the one about how you better get Wildroot Cream Oil, Charlie, it's made with soothing Lanolin. What ever happened to Wildroot? Or Lanolin? Or, for that matter, Charlie?

We arrived at the landing and unlocked the boat, and Mr. White took his place in the bow, Mr. Southam in the engine room and I in the place of honor at the stern. Part of my duty was to shove us off, and I did it with such a will we were propelled almost to the middle of the lake. Now, it was the duty of the man at the oars to see that the oars indeed were aboard before casting off, and this Mr. Southam had neglected to do, although in the subsequent discussion he allowed as how I might well have seen to it, since I was the last man on the shore. Mr. Southam being my employer, I refrained from replying to him in the same tone as his remarks to me, and Mr. White intervened, in any case, saying that, as the man in the bow, it appeared to be his duty to propel us back to the dock, which he did.

The oars being retrieved from their hiding place in the bush, we proceeded to fish Forgie from end to end and side to side, with only the occasional trout as our reward, so when we lunched, it was in silence, which seemed to suit all three of us well enough, there being no point in going back over the incident of the oars, much less the manner of stopping the Jeep at the bottom of that hill. Dick White opined that maybe the day was too bright for fishing, and I agreed a bit of overcast might help, and that was about it until we tidied up and doused our fire and agreed to head back down the trail.

Down we went, the descent of the Forgie portage being easier and faster than climbing up. We sculled across Bowie and found ourselves back at Percival, with my companions saying we might as well head straight back, when I decided to disclose the secret information.

"I have reason to believe," said I, "that, if we cast a fly into those lily pads, there are fish there."

"Well," said Mr. White, "Maybe if we were fishing for bass there might be something, but I never heard of trout like that."

"Sounds crazy to me," said Mr. Southam, "but what the hell."

It was agreed I should make first try, so I unlimbered the fly rod and drew a bead on a tiny speck of clear water in the middle of the lily pads.

The fly fell gently towards the tiny opening, but it didn't get there. It was within a handsbreadth of landing when a streak of black, silver and red rose from the water to meet it, and that trout hit so heavily it hooked itself. Down into the weeds it splashed, and I horsed it out of the lily pads so hard it would have left the water, had it not been so big and strong. My fish was no sooner in the boat than Mr. White took his turn, and had one on his first cast. Same size as mine, what in today's parlance would be called a kilo. Southam cast, with the same result. Three casts into the lilies, three fish.

So it went, for what seemed like half an hour, but may have been more like fifteen minutes, in the course of which we made a wreckage of that lily patch, but filled our creels. They were still taking when we passed our limit, and it was agreed that my next cast would be the last, as indeed it was. Same pattern—fly barely on the water when it was taken—same deep tug, same heavy pressure to get the trout into open water. And when he came this time, there was a big piece of wood attached to the line, fastened by the twining stems of the lilies.

At the Magannassippi Club, it is the custom of members to carry a wooden club with which to dispatch trout in sporting fashion, by hitting them over the head. I had never acquired one of these "priests," as they were called in the angling catalogues, preferring to snap the trout's head back and break its neck, a process viewed as repulsive by some members, because of the tendency of the trout to emit a spew of blood at the moment of breakage, spotting the clothing of anybody sitting or standing in my vicinity.

Mr. Southam eyed my trout, coming in with the stick of wood attached, and he shouted, "He's bringing in his own priest!"

So we netted the trout and the stick, and I did the honors by wielding the weapon and stunning the trout, which was exactly the same size as the others. We all agreed we had never seen such a catch in so short a time, or so strange a place. I divulged the source of my information, and we agreed the Americans weren't such bad fellows, after all, especially if they happened to love dogs.

When we got back to the Jeep we were filled with wonder, and we stood for a few minutes after everything was stowed, taking in the scene and wondering, not if anybody would believe us, but whether we should tell about it at all. We agreed that, for the good of future fishing in Percival, we might as well keep quiet, apart from thanking our American benefactor.

Then Dick White said a remarkable thing.

Not a man normally given to fancy talk, he uttered these words. "By Monday, the trailing arbutus will bloom on the Forgie portage."

I wasn't sure I had heard him correctly, and asked what he had said.

"By Monday, the trailing arbutus will bloom on the Forgie portage."

"Amazing," said I.

"What's so bloody amazing?" asked Mr. Southam, taking his place at the wheel.

"Dick has just uttered one of the most beautiful lines I've ever heard," I said.

"What line?" asked the puzzled Mr. White.

"You said that, by Monday, the trailing arbutus will bloom on the Forgie portage."

"So it will," said Mr. White.

"Of course it will," said Mr. Southam. "What's so bloody amazing about that?"

"The words, the words," said I. "Feel the rhythm of them— sheer poetry."

"My ass," said Mr. Southam, starting the engine and drowning out further thought.

So we returned to camp, and we didn't tell the others, and I entered Dick White's line in the club log, where it remains to this day, a source of puzzlement to most, and of pleasure to some. I have asked him to attempt a second line to the poem, but he never has.

ANGLING
WITH M.D.S

Medical doctors make good angling companions, though they are inclined to talk a lot.

Not about medicine. On the water, doctors never talk about medicine at all. Indeed, it has been my experience they don't talk much about it in their offices, preferring to discuss the politics of the day until the closing five minutes of the visit, when they stop asking about the news, and start giving it, along with the usual caution to lose weight and stop drinking.

Doctors make good anglers because they are inclined to be useful with their hands. Surgeons are the best of

all, but they, too, talk a lot when they are fishing, I assume because they get to talk so little when they are operating. They
also have good memories, schooled as they are not to leave
tools or sponges inside their patients before they sew them up.
A surgeon's way with monofilament is a delight to behold, and
their hands don't tremble the way others do, especially if the
fish are biting.

Because of their dexterity, it has always seemed to me that
women make better anglers, knot in and knot out, than men,
and it has always puzzled me that there are not more women
fishing, because they are naturals in almost every facet of the
art. I am equally at a loss to explain why there are not more
women surgeons (or chefs for that matter), and I am told it is
lack of opportunity—great surgeons and chefs come up
through channels that have been male-dominated for so long
there is no chance of a woman reaching the pinnacle of achieve-
ment and acclaim. People have to want to hire them, and when
you are going under the knife, you become very selective, especially if you are rich.

Physicians enjoy a special popularity in fishing parties, and
the larger the party, the more likely there will be one or two
doctors along. This has given the medical profession an edge in
invitations to the choicest fishing waters, the simple reason
being that the wealthy people who control those waters are inclined to have assorted ailments, and it is handy to have someone along who can act as a sort of combat medical station,
administering treatment in the field, pending either healing or
evacuation.

Not all the accidents on fishing trips have to do with fishing, because the nights can yield some incidents that call for
medical attention.

Anglers of a certain age, for instance, have to rise during the
night to relieve their bladders, which they usually do off the
front steps of the lodge, sometimes three or four abreast. In such
circumstances, widdlers have been known to lose their footing,
especially if there is no moon, and suffer injuries in the fall.

At my favorite fishing club, the way to relief in the night
lay at the end of the hall, where a door opened onto a four-foot
drop with a rock below, known as Pissing Rock. Generations of
anglers had anointed this rock to the point where it gleamed
when the moon was full, whether it was wet or not, and it

usually was, depending on how many members were in camp. Sure enough, one night after much roistering, a member took one step too many and hurtled onto the pissing rock below, uttering piercing cries that I can still hear in my dreams. There was a doctor in the house, and all injuries proved superficial, except to the dignity of the fallen.

On another occasion, and another camp, there was a casualty at the president's annual dinner, held to mark the opening of the trout season.

Thirty of us were gathered at a big U-shaped table in the dining room, and everything was going swimmingly until one member took offence at something he thought another member had said.

The offended party happened to be Carol Hardinge, Viscount Hardinge of Lahore, a mighty man in Montréal social and business circles, horse owner and sportsman extraordinaire, who was valued as a club member because he always brought goodies from the Ritz Carlton in Montréal, of which he was a part-owner. We called his pate "meat loaf," but we ate it anyway, and we drank the champagne he brought in cases, and we put up with his insistence on a separate bedroom because, he said, he couldn't stand the snoring of others. He himself snored like a buzzsaw, so isolating him wasn't all that much of a hardship.

This evening, late in the dinner, His Lordship rose to his feet in wrath and said he had heard a discouraging word about Her Majesty the Queen, and not from an American member, either. It was a Canadian who had voiced indifference to the Crown, and Hardinge said such conduct was not to be tolerated, whereupon he invited the assembled members to rise and drink the loyal toast to Her Majesty.

All rose, and drank a dollop of Hardinge's champagne, whereupon he hurled his crystal goblet, the club's finest, in the huge fireplace that dominated the dining room.

At least, he intended the goblet for the fireplace. In his wrought-up state, he hooked his shot, and the goblet flew off at right angles, imbedding itself in the bald pate of an unoffending member who, so far as anybody knew, had not uttered a word throughout the entire dinner.

The crystal shattered, and the blood gushed in a most alarming manner, whereupon two medical doctors who were in the company rushed to the aid of the stricken and ordered him laid out in the lounge, where treatment was administered. The flow of blood was stanched, stitches were applied and the victim was able to return to the table, wearing a turban and saying he held no grudges. Viscount Hardinge of Lahore, filled with remorse, absented himself from table and retired to his room upstairs, sending down a note putting in his resignation as a member of the club, with apologies all round. A delegation was dispatched to the upper regions, and Hardinge was persuaded to withdraw his resignation, being assured that all was forgiven. I have always thought it was that we couldn't stand the thought of no more meat loaf or champagne—a fate that eventually befell the club when Hardinge died with his waders on, flogging the waters of his favorite Québec salmon river, and I can still hear his mumbled advice. "Always go first class, my boy." Easy enough for him to say.

But today's topic is doctors as anglers, and thereby hangs a tale.

The isolation that is one of fishing's attractions can complicate the practice of medicine and lead to improvisation of tools and techniques, such as the time two distinguished surgeons used an apple and a knothole to save the eye of a prominent lawyer.

If you don't wear protective glasses while fishing, you will after you hear this story. Either that, or make sure the leading surgeons of the United States and Great Britain are somewhere within reach, with their thinking caps on.

My favorite medical angler is Dr. Allen Boydon, longtime professor of surgery at the University of Oregon Medical School in Portland who, with his wife Marjorie, has fished the upper reaches of the Rogue River for as long as either of them can remember.

The river is Rogue by name and rogue by nature, swirling as it does through canyons carved through the Klamath range of the Cascade Mountains. The river is white water from Grant's Pass to where it empties into the Pacific at Gold Beach, and though Interstate 5 crosses it at Grant's Pass, and coastal route 101 at Gold Beach, it maintains much of the wilderness feel it had when Zane Grey made it famous.

Allan and Kathleen Boydon treasure the river for its isolation and for the steelhead trout that migrate upstream each year, offering some of the best fly fishing to be had anywhere in North America, when you hit the run. Near the headwaters of the river is Crater Lake National Park, and east of that spreads the wasteland of the Great Sandy Desert.

The Boydons entertain guests from all over the world during the fishing season, and on this occasion the visiting angler was Mr. Philip Allison, Regis Professor of Surgery at Oxford University. They had good fishing the first three days, so good they prolonged their stay for a full week. On the last day, they were taking their final casts when one of the upriver guides, Prince Helfrich, came downriver looking for "The Doc," shouting that there was a medical emergency, up at Tyee Bay.

Portland lawyer Frank Spears, a friend of the Boydons, had been hooked in the left eye by a hair-tied streamer fly on a number eight hook, and the barb was buried in the color of the iris, both chambers of the eye being filled with blood.

Boydon and Allison exchanged glances, and established that neither had done any eye surgery. Boydon had a small case of instruments at his cottage, and some novocaine. Before heading upriver, he and Allison conferred on how they might proceed. Night was falling, and it would be dark when they reached the victim—the guide said there were flashlights at the scene, the ones they used for jacklighting deer. From Boydon's supply of flies he picked one that resembled the fly in Spears's eye—a Royal Coachman bucktail with hairs of black bear.

"One more thing," said Boydon. "We'll need a piece of wood with a knothole."

"And we'd better get an apple," said Allison.

Boydon beamed, getting the idea. "A soft apple, something like the texture of an eye."

They had apples in camp, and the two surgeons selected one that they thought came closest to the texture they were looking for. In the remaining light, as the guide motored them upstream, they practiced manipulating the hook in the apple, knowing that the eye is a globe with water in it, and that, if they pulled the hook through, it would leave two holes in the eyeball and scramble the eye. And too much pressure would pull the eye out of its socket.

To do all this in a moving boat, the two surgeons inserted the apple into the knothole, resembling the way a human eye sits in its socket. Boydon held the board with the apple in the hole while Allison fiddled with the hook, and they they changed places. A couple of times, they tore the flesh of the apple and had to roll it around in the knothole to begin again. By the time they reached the afflicted angler, they had their moves plotted, having punctured most of the apple, and scarred the knothole more than somewhat.

"We were soaking wet when we got there, just worrying about it," says Dr. Boydon, who had done combat surgery during the war and is one of the calmest men imaginable, in any circumstance.

At the Tyee Bay camp, they were greeted by proprietor Halley Witherwax and riverman Red Keller, who reported the patient was distinctly uncomfortable. Boydon and Allison went to work at once, using the fly in the apple as their model—save the pulp, save the eye. They snipped the hook, extracted it, bandaged both Spears's eyes and shipped him downriver to the settlement of Marial on an illegal mining claim, where there was a Jeep, which drove the patient sixty miles to Medford accompanied by Allison, who was making notes on the wilderness operation. From Medford, Spears was flown to Portland, where ophonologist Bob Fischer took over.

The eye was saved and lawyer Spears has full use of it, thanks to the fluke of having two leading surgeons fishing the Rogue at the right time and the right place.

"It sort of knocked the fishing out of our minds," says Boydon today, "but Allison said it was the best he ever had."

MY SON
THE JUDGE

I had been glad for this son in some good moments, but never a better one than this.

There had been the baseball, the hits, the running catches, the long, smart throws from deep right field.

And the touchdowns, the girls draped on his shoulder pads, and the time he cracked two helmets, hitting the line in a game they lost.

The appointment to the bench and the occasional tidings of judgments wiser than his years.

A father's admiration is said to be nine parts envy, but the only thing

I ever envied him was where he lived, in the prettiest small city in the land, overlooking the great river that haunts the dreams of all who have ever lived by it, or even known it.

He didn't talk much about dreams, at least not to his father, and he was tough enough to have settled battles with his fists, once taking on an entire railroad car of navy men, who were harassing a University of New Brunswick classmate on the Ocean Limited, and another time rooting out some ruffians who had harassed his grandfather, and leaving them on the ground for dead. He played fullback for the varsity football team at U.N.B. and smashed two helmets in a single game, hitting the line. He also blew all his subjects in that freshman year because of sports and, on being given a second chance, he abandoned the field for the books, and made it into law, leaving for legend a schoolboy soccer game with his brother playing for the other school. The brother, whose nickname was "Animal," fell to the turf, groaning in agony, and this son kicked the fallen brother with a laugh, and told the referee, "He's faking."

He led a group of players to England, for a midwinter tournament against teams in the Midlands, and they came back as walking wounded, with a taste for English beer and probably girls as well. In a track meet, he fell on the cinders in the last lap and rose to finish, giving his team the needed point to win, and then went to hospital for three hours on the operating table, while they dug the cinders out of him.

He stammered until he was thirteen years old, and at age nine, there was a diagnosis of a hole in his heart, his heart being half again as big as it should have been. When his lymph glands were suspect at that age, he gave away all his possessions and said goodbye, but he wasn't to go yet.

All these things he did, along with a lot we didn't know about, and the police only came to the house once, when he was accused of throwing a chocolate milk shake on a black man, and got off with an apology.

He wore his shirttail out even when he was Clerk of the Legislature, and once, when advising the Speaker on a point of procedure, he relieved himself in the Speaker's sink, continuing to advise as he did so.

The Judge

He once asked his father what was the best piece of ass he had ever had, a question few fathers could handle on firm ground. Another time, he said playing and landing a salmon was "better than coming. Not better than fucking, but better than coming." When his mother and I parted, he came after me in a hotel room and called me a son of a bitch, not exactly the appropriate epithet, given the circumstances. Then he held me out the hotel window by my feet, before pulling me back in and saying we would discuss the matter no further. And, for the rest of our time together, we did not.

He fished hard when he got into it, and there were good times and bad on the St. John and Miramichi. He got the bug when he organized a spring trip for the two of us, and we came back with what looked like a fine catch of salmon, caught trolling on the big bucktail flies they use on the early fish, but my father was there, and he looked at them disdainfully and said: "Slinks!" Black salmon, that is, the ones that had spent the winter in the river.

"Taste like blotting paper," he said, and when we cooked them, they did—Father had a turn of phrase like that. While exploring a brook, he once was chased by a farmer's dog "so cross he skinned his teeth right back to his pecker!"

When you fish in New Brunswick, you hear a lot of expressions like that, and this son made a collection of them, which he used in some of his judgments from the bench, including his scorn for a senior judge who had ruled that a women's breasts had no more sexual significance than a man's whiskers. That judge, said our son in a much-publicized ruling, must never have been there, and by upsetting the higher court he got into the law books.

Fishing with him had its perils—companions tended to be in awe of the judge until he took part in a contest that involved setting fire to farts, in which he explained that it was important to do it through your underwear, to avoid igniting bumfuzz. The resulting bursts of flame were known as Blue Angels. In another fit of frenzy, he tried to ram an Absorbine Jr. bottle into a special and sensitive part of his father's anatomy.

A vulgar bully? It sounds like it, except that he always managed to leave the impression that he didn't mean it, and that, for him, abuse was a form of endearment, a tendency not uncommon in New Brunswick men, and tolerated by the women who love them. (Hello there, Maureen!)

There was a gentler side—the collection of tin toys, the trading in duck and goose decoys, the buying and selling of old magazines, the obsession with garage sales that caused him to turn in his credit cards because the bank account was always empty. He had a keen eye for antiques and a fine sense of price. He planted and operated a prize apple orchard, and hosted a historic '50s nostalgia party featuring his singing of *Splish Splash*. On the bench, he was known for his compassion for local Indians who came before him, and won their respect for punishment that fit the crimes of drunkenness and fishing violations, with the emphasis on community service. Once, a young man named Fequet came before him on a minor theft charge, and Judge Lynch identified him as being from Old Fort and arranged to pay his way home. He rescued a Miramichi drunk and turned him into his fishing guide, philosopher and friend. Blake's siblings came to him for comfort when they were afflicted, as did his mother, and he provided healing, shelter and sustenance, if not T.L.C.

When he was Clerk of the New Brunswick Legislature, he also ran the province's legal aid system. He was no churchgoer, yet he was a warden of Christ Church Cathedral and helped keep it solvent. He played a big hand in the development of the King's Landing Heritage Village. When he walked along the streets of Fredericton, half the people greeted him by name— "Blake"—and he seemed to know everybody, including all who had appeared before him as defendants.

A paradox? Certainly—back to the fishing.

Once, when we were fishing fast water on the Old Fort and he had caught his day's limit of salmon, he taunted me from his resting place on the bank. Thus goaded, I ventured into deeper water than intended, and with my feet on slippery rocks I appealed for help, before the water foamed over the top of my chest waders and I would be gone.

"Repeat after me," intoned the judge, whose legal education I had paid for, and against whom I had never spoken a cross word. "I, Charles Lynch, being of sound mind, do leave all my worldly possessions to my son, Blake."

"Bastard," I said, struggling my way to shore just to spite him.

What are strong arms for, unless to help a father in distress?

I had seen him swing baseball bats with them, and throw to home plate from the outfield, and win fist fights.

I had even, in what may have been his most prodigious feat of strength (harking back to his Uncle Harry, and Grandfather Mahoney, who were legends when it came to heaving people and things around), hold a fully powered outboard motor in his hands and keep the boat on course at the same time.

Honestly.

This was on the St. John River, on the Hartt salmon pool within view of his house on the hill, and he had explained when we started out that, once he got the motor running, he wasn't going to turn it off until we got to our appointed spot, because it was a devil to start.

He got it started, all right, and away we went, but there was some terrible profanity from the stern and, when I turned around, there he was, holding the motor in his hands, and it still running.

The stern post in the old rowboat was rotten and, as soon as it felt the strain of the outboard, it came apart. With nothing to fasten the motor to the boat, my son was cradling it in his arms. I kept shouting for him to turn it off, and he said to hell with that, he would never get it going again, and it was in that mode that we made our way through the water, with his arms taking

the full thrust of the power, and managing to keep us on course at the same time. At least, I assumed it was the course. When we got there and he turned the motor off and we fished, there was nothing doing, and later we were able to get a tow back home. I asked him if he juggled chain saws as a sideline, but there was no reply. I can't remember what horsepower that motor was, but I think it was a five.

And once, when the fishing was good, he was sitting in the middle of the salmon pool, hunched over in conversation with the guide while the fish were rising all around.

"Get your line in, dammit!" I roared.

A disdainful look, and, "We're changing flies, fart face!"

There is no protocol for a fatherly reply when thus addressed, and when he got the right fly on he landed a nice fish, but I can still feel the sting of his scorn.

The great moment came on the last day of a week-long foray on our favorite Québec wilderness river. The plane was coming for us at noon, and he elected to have one more go at the top pool, which was about forty-five minutes from camp, most of it straight up.

The climb is rough, featuring a swamp that we called the "socksucker," because its mucky depths could suck the socks off your feet inside your waders. Guides could sprint across it without sinking in, and occasional young anglers could keep pace.

Up he went to that prettiest pool in all the world, studded with rocks, the water moving in riffs and swirls and bits of foam, every one of them signalling a possible resting place of a salmon. People who have seen that pool carry the memory of it with them for the rest of their lives, and wherever they fish, use it as their point of comparison, even if they have never taken a fish there. There are two rocks about five meters from shore that provide the perfect roosts for anglers, and it was on one of these that he stood, unreeled his line and started to cast.

He had an hour before heading back to camp for the rendezvous with the plane, and forty-five minutes passed with no action on the wet flies he was using. As a last resort, he tied on his favorite dry White Wulff, a big fuzzy one he had bought from a Newfoundland fly-tier on the trip in. It resembled a sheep in need of shearing, but the hunch was there.

After all, it was in this same pool that his father had taken the only salmon of the day, on the most ridiculous fly ever to touch these hallowed waters, a thing that had been sent by an angler in Calgary, Alberta, where they take rainbow trout from the Bow River in the shadow of the oilpatch skyscrapers. This fly had evidently been put together out of bristles from a scrubbing brush, held in place by pink yarn from an old dressing gown, and the whole thing coated with globs of glue. "Just one cast," father had said, and he launched the abomination into the stream. *Wham!* came the salmon, and everybody marvelled and laughed, and the fly was christened the Bow Belle, and given an honored place on the den wall at home.

The White Wulff was wafted across the water and dropped through the still air like a leaf, ready to start its drift downstream. Out of the water to meet it came the salmon of the day, of the trip, of the season, of a lifetime. As the son described it, *"Ka-ZOOM!"* followed by *"Ke-POW."* With a waving of the arms he would re-enact the spray, and the whine of the reel as the fish made its first run, and then the arc of the jump, the splash, the flash of silver and the rod bent double.

He returned to camp with that salmon, and the look on his face is with me still. It was the memory of that fish that obsessed him with the sport, and led to so many forays on the St. John and the Miramichi, the acquisition of a house on the Southwest Miramichi with fishing rights, and a collection of antique fly rods that became the talk of the river.

It was there on the Miramichi that he fished as long as he could stand, fighting the cancer that spread from his melanoma lesion—he killed his last salmon two weeks before he called in sick on a Tuesday, and died on the Thursday. Father got there half an hour before he died, still looking as strong in body as ever, but gasping his final breaths away.

At the memorial service, the whole town turned out and everybody wept and, when the choir and congregation lit into quick-tempo versions of *The Battle Hymn* and *Onward, Christian Soldiers*, father cried hardest of all and thought of the top pool that would see this young fisherman no more.

FLIES FOR NEW ZEALAND

W hen the bug bites really deep, anglers get inter-ested in tying flies, which is more related to the jeweller's art than to things fishy. It happened to my son the judge and, in the last years of his life, he filled the house up with the stuff of fly-tying, including skeins of yarns and bunches of feathers and all kinds of hair and hooks and tin-sel, together with the vice that becomes the scene of the action when fly-tying is afoot.

So it was that he became ex-cited when his youngest sister, Lucinda, telephoned from Ottawa to say she was going to New Zealand, in her capacity of press secretary to the Minister for International Trade, Pat Carney, who, in concert with our friend Simon Reisman, was midway through negotiating the Free Trade Agreement with the United States.

The Taupo Trade Ministers Conference was to be attended by trade ministers from twenty-two developed and developing countries, who would discuss multilateral trading issues. But what was important to Blake was that his sister would be going to Lake Taupo, in the center of the big North Island, and boasting the best fly fishing in the world for trout. His voice, normally the lazy drawl peculiar to New Brunswickers, with a low singsong cadence, picked up to a high pitch when he described the joys that would await his baby sister, and he said he would get to work that very night creating, with his own hands, some flies for her to use when she went fishing.

He had just finished reading a book about the psyche of the Taupo trout and promised to send her off with some guaranteed winners, based on patterns from the book—as luck would have it, he had all the makings for the Taupo flies.

Cindy reminded him that she had never been fly fishing in her life, and that her minister's schedule was such it was most unlikely she would get a spare moment. He would not hear of it, and went into a rhapsody of what he had heard about the size of the lake, the size of the trout, the location of the best waters, and the assurance that she was in for the greatest experience of her life, including himself.

Within a week, a package arrived by courier at Minister Carney's office in the External Affairs building, addressed to Ms Cindy Boucher. Wrapped with care in a blue Birk's box were six brightly colored flies and a note wishing his sister luck, together with a demand for a full report on her return. Little Sister gave the package to her secretary and asked her to be sure to include it in her briefcase of material destined for New Zealand. (Father's note—mistake number one, breaking the first rule of angling, which is always to tend to your own gear, trusting nobody, be they mates, secretaries, friends or airline agents. There are times when you have to give in to the latter, and there is no tension quite like seeing one's rods disappear through the floppy baggage doors, nor is there greater relief than seeing them turn up at the remote airports frequented by anglers. But no power on earth would ever lead me to entrust reels or flies to the care of another, because if all else goes astray, you can always raise a rod in fishing country.)

The Carney delegation would be away for seven days, including travel time, in the course of which she would do the Taupo conference, go on to Wellington for meetings with Prime Minister David Lange, and then to Canberra for meetings with Prime Minister Bob Hawke. Carney had a speech to the Canberra Press Club, and then on to Brisbane to announce Canada's participation in Expo '88.

Given the fact that Carney had been voted one of the toughest bosses in Canada to work for, the prospects of her press secretary getting in any fishing were not bright.

The delegation had a big baggage load, from briefing books to secure fax machines, so External Affairs arranged for an office to be set up in a motel in Taupo, so all would be ready when they arrived.

The House of Commons was in session, with the U.S. trade negotiations being raised daily in Question Period, with both Minister Carney and Ambassador Reisman on the hot seat. Carney had to be kept informed.

Carney and her staff flew from Ottawa to Vancouver for the first leg of the trip, and then were to proceed by commercial carrier to Auckland, via Honolulu.

Somewhere over the Pacific, on the flight from Vancouver to Honolulu, Ms Boucher opened her briefcase to look for the flies her brother had tied for her so lovingly. Alas, they were nowhere to be found. The secretary, in the flurry before departure, had neglected to pack them. The press secretary was accustomed to facing an aroused Carney, but how would she explain this to the Judge?

The delegation had a fifteen-hour stopover in Honolulu, so immediately on arrival, Ms Boucher called back to Ottawa and told her secretary, somewhat curtly, that there was only one last hope for the flies. Dr. Sylvia Ostry, the prime minister's personal representative for the Economic Summit, was leaving Ottawa to join the Carney delegation in Honolulu and go on to Auckland with them. The word was that Ostry had already left for the Ottawa airport, but the secretary would do her best. Little Sister sweated profusely until Dr. Ostry arrived and joined the party at a seafood restaurant for dinner, before the 1:30 a.m. takeoff for Auckland.

The minister's press secretary leapt to her feet and cried, "Did you bring my flies?"

"Your what?" queried the learned doctor, peering over her bifocals.

"My flies! Have you got my flies?"

It is not the sort of query learned economists are accustomed to hearing on their way to international conferences, and Dr. Ostry's look conveyed the impression she thought Ms Boucher had been into the Mai Tai, as indeed was the case.

"I know nothing about flies," she said with a wrinkle of her nose, "but I do have something here—some hysterical woman chased after me as I was leaving for the airport, and insisted that it be delivered to the minister's staff in Honolulu."

She reached into her bag and produced a small package with Ms Boucher's name on it.

Cindy ripped it open and kissed the contents—there were the flies, custom tied in Fredericton, N.B. for the taking of trout in Lake Taupo, N.Z.

During the fourteen-hour flight from Hawaii, Cindy Boucher dreamed wild dreams, which was not unusual for her, except that, for this one and only time, the dreams were of fish.

It was a four-hour drive from Auckland to Lake Taupo, and once there, Minister Carney was dropped off at what was billed as the most luxurious resort in the Southern Hemisphere, Huka Lodge. As luck would have it, the staff continued on to a motel overlooking Lake Taupo itself, a few hundred feet from the main wharf. The minister's press secretary immediately started to plot her escape upon the waters.

She could see the anglers from her motel window. The whole place was geared to fish—people talked of little else, there were brochures in the rooms outlining how to get fishing. Cindy opened the box of flies and spread them out on her dresser.

Alas, though, there was a summons from the minister.

There were receptions to attend, and the actual meeting was taking place five miles inland from the hotel. At the Huka Lodge, ice carvers had made crystal sculptures of giant trout.

The spouses' itinerary for the duration of the conference consisted entirely of fishing—"Guaranteed to be the experience of your life."

But all members of the delegation had to be on call for Carney, and were forbidden to leave the conference center. There were speeches to write, proposals to edit, and press releases to be issued, and Cindy was put in charge of conveying Canada's proposal on agriculture to the international media, when she wanted to think only of fish.

At night, due to the time change, she was on the phone to the Canadian media back home, trying to solicit coverage for her minister, and faxing the press releases.

The last morning of the conference, she stared with bleary eyes at the flies on her bureau. She collected the morning papers and laughed hollowly at the coverage—the front page stories all dealt with the trophy trout caught by the spouses, and there was a big picture of one Commonwealth wife holding up a dozen of the beauties. There was barely a mention of the business transacted by ministers at the conference.

Cindy was waiting for the daily fax from Ottawa with secret instructions, together with the press clippings that would tell if there had been any of the coveted coverage back home.

But the secret fax machine remained silent, while the staff went ahead with a press release and the speech for Carney in Canberra, as well as the briefing book for the minister's meeting with the Prime Minister of New Zealand.

Lucinda called Ottawa, and they said the fax had been sent—all twenty-four pages of it. Alarm bells went off at the thought that it had been sent somewhere else by mistake.

Cindy was still on the phone when there was a knock at the motel door. When it was opened, there stood a fisherman in full regalia—waders, vest, hat and all. He asked if this was the Canadian delegation, and when Cindy said it was, he handed over the twenty-four-page fax, which had landed in the office on the fisherman's wharf.

"I thought it might be important," he said.

"You got that right," said she, adding as an afterthought, "How's the fishing?"

"Never better," he said. "We guarantee fish, no ifs, ands or buts. You must try it."

A quiet sob from Cindy, who says the only thing that cheered her up was a press clipping in the fax package—Canadian Press had bitten on one of her telephone briefings and put out a lengthy story about Canada's contribution at the conference. At least, the minister would be pleased about that.

But, no. On the plane to Wellington, Pat Carney read the story and blew up. They had the facts right, but the name wrong. The reporter chose to use Cindy Boucher's name a dozen times in the piece, when what was wanted was the name of Carney.

"Press secretaries," snapped the minister, "are not supposed to get their names in the press."

"I should have gone fishing," says Cindy, a thought with which her brother, on being informed later, agreed.

VICEROYS AND ESKIMOS

The most silent of all fishing companions are Eskimos. Call them Inuit, if they prefer—I have never had one of them express a preference, certainly not when we were together in their homeland, the Arctic.

So disinclined are they to conversation that it has made me suspicious of the accounts of early explorers (intruders, in today's parlance), who told tall tales of coming upon Eskimo encampments and, in a single night, hearing the stories, histories and legends of that particular band, in addition to enjoying hospitality so complete it included the rubbing of noses and much else, besides. I suspect they would have been lucky to get more than a few smiles and grunts, and made the rest up.

My solution to Eskimo silence has been to tell them stories, or sing them songs, or play them tunes on the mouth organ, all of which they seem to appreciate. I should say that, when they are called upon to perform for white visitors, many Eskimos do so with a will, dancing and drumming and uttering gutteral cries, to the growing excitement of all who behold the spectacle, especially other Eskimos. It has always been my practice to respond with a return performance, something few white visitors seem inclined to do, and a tendency that earned me the title in the north of "The Pipe That Talks."

On one visit to Bathurst Inlet Lodge, I told the proprietor that I had had my fill of the bird-watching and muskox-spotting that was the lodge's specialty, and would enjoy some fishing.

There was an idle aircraft in camp that day, and it was arranged to fly me to a spot a hundred kilometers away on the Huguetuk River, which had only been fished once before in human memory.

The anglers on that occasion were Governor General Roly Michener and his principal secretary, Esmond Butler, and their accounts of the fishing became part of the Arctic lore, scarcely to be believed by those who had not been there, and could never get there.

One of the local Eskimo band was delegated to come along, and away we flew, with X marking the spot on the map where the fishing was, at the bottom of a long rapid where the Upper Huguetuk flowed into the Lower.

The pilot let us off at the appointed spot and said he would be back in three hours. He also left us a big galvanized wash tub for the catch, which I thought was optimistic, as creels go.

I had brought a spinning rod and a fly rod, and elected to try the fly rod first, though the Eskimo guide shook his head, indicating a preference for the stouter spinner.

He pointed to a rock where I could stand, and after a couple of false casts, I put the fly on the water and started to retrieve it. This resulted in a spectacle the like of which I have never seen—surging waves as several fish came in pursuit, a sight so riveting I stopped retrieving the line. In an instant, there was the most terrible tug, and away went the fly and the line, the reel screeching as the fish ran.

It took me ten minutes to bring that fish to the net, and when my companion had it in the tub he gave me a dubious look, tapping his watch and pointing to the single fish. I got the message that my job was to fill the tub, and that the spinning rod was the right tool for the work. No matter—I had to try the fly again, and again the scene was the same. This time, it took me fifteen minutes to bring the fish to shore, another lake trout of about the same size, five kilos. Again, a shake of the Eskimo head.

I did one more cast when the fly, just to see that bow wave coming after it, and when we landed that one—a char this time—I agreed to switch rods, and my friend resumed his smile. I had a plain silver lure, onto which I stuck some red plastic from Canadian Tire, and the result was total. One cast, one fish—in an hour, the tub was half full. And then the rain came—we had a little pup tent in which we took refuge, and I invited my companion to tell me something of his life.

Grunt.

I told him something of mine.

Grunt.

I played him a tune.

Grunt.

Sang him a song.

Grunt.

And so we passed the time, congenially enough, except that any conversation there was, was mine. I am willing to admit that, had we been operating in his language, things might have been more loquacious, though I found out back at camp that he was perfectly at home in English.

When the rain stopped, we resumed fishing and, by the time the plane came back for us, the tub was full, and it took the pilot, my guide and myself to carry it from the fishing spot to where the plane was moored. We weighed the catch when we got back to camp and it came to over 100 kilos, which in pre-metric terms was about 250 pounds. There were a lot of people in camp, so the fish were put to good use, right down to the last fin, and the residue fed the dogs.

That was the beginning of my fishing adventures in the Arctic, which included one more visit to that magic spot on the Huguetuk, of which more later.

The only emperor we have ever had in Canada was Stuart Hodgson, the man who moved the seat of government from Ottawa to Yellowknife and proceeded to govern the whole vast Northwest Territories as a personal fief, outraging many, but pleasing most.

Among the many decrees of Emperor Hodgson was that there should be established an organization to be known as the Franklin Probe, dedicated to the search for the bones of John Franklin and his men, who had disappeared without trace in their search for the Northwest Passage, thus giving rise to one of the greatest of the white man's legends, though the Eskimos never thought much of it, and do not to this day.

It was Hodgson's thought that the romance of the Arctic needed emphasis, to counter all the pros and cons of development of resources, native land claims and the evils of white government. He seized on the Franklin story and made it his own, recruiting various and sundry interested parties, including myself as media scribe and principal fisherman.

It was to the latter task that I bent my best efforts, to the point where Hodgson and the rest of the party, wherever we went in the search for Franklin's bones, depended on me to bring supper—and usually it worked. We had lots of other rations, because it was not Hodgon's way to scrimp, and we used to say that, when his term of office in the north was finished, we wanted to stick around for the Royal Commission investigation, which frustrated bureaucrats in Ottawa were sure to launch. They never did, in fact, and the extremes to which Hodgson went to bring democratic ways to the north have never been laid bare, probably because he had more on them than they had on him.

The angling chores that fell to me were mostly in salt water, off gravel beaches, including Fury Beach on the Boothia Peninsula, the only part of mainland Canada named after a brand of gin. (The gin family used part of their earnings from the booze to sponsor exploration, hence the Booth label on our northernmost extremity.) The wreck of HMS Fury took place on this beach, and much of her cargo remained stashed on the shore—anchors, chains, cables, barrels of nails, all things that 150 years of Arctic weather had scarcely rusted, since everything lasts forever in those arid, frozen climes.

My favored lure for the work was the Mepps Black Fury, Number 4, the one with the yellow dots on the black spinner. I do not recall using any other hardware in the Arctic salt water, and it was death on any Arctic char within range, which usually meant a decent cast from shore. No worry about snags, nothing to impede casting except spectators on shore, shouting encouragement.

Fishing for the pot is purposeful work, especially when the Eskimo guides are waiting behind the angler for the next fish, and they have the stove going and the pan sizzling and everybody is hungry.

On one occasion, at Pelly Bay, I started bringing them in on every cast, lovely char of the kind southern gourmets dream about. And, as fast as I flung the fish up on the gravel, the Eskimos grabbed them and did their filleting, which seemed to me a very wasteful procedure, since it was our practice to serve and eat the whole fish. The Eskimos had knives as sharp as razors, and with two strokes they took a fillet off each side of the backbone and threw the rest away. It was these fillets that we ate, the Eskimos indicating that the rest of the fish, the belly, the tail section, and the part near the head, were unfit for human consumption. I never did find out if they were assuming the white eaters to be fastidious, or whether it really was their habit to eat only the choice fillets of fish. I only know they threw away more of the fish than we ate, but it didn't matter, because I fished until my arms ached, and everybody had their fill, and all agreed that Arctic char, filleted and cooked within seconds of being landed, were out of this world.

There were days when I skunked, and Hodgson, no angler himself, assumed the famine had something to do with me, insisting I must be doing something wrong. Nothing would convince him the fish were not wherever he decreed them to be, every time and all the time.

There came a time when we were back at Bathurst Inlet Lodge, and who should fly in but Governor General Edward Schreyer and party, which meant a vice-regal reception from the local Eskimo community, and a bash that raged far into the night, to the delight of the Schreyer party.

Early next day, His Excellency expressed a desire for some fishing, and Hodgson immediately nominated me as the guide, whereupon I suggested the Huguetuk, a river to which I had never expected to return.

The vice-regal aircraft being available (it was an army Twin Otter, with a crew of eight) we set off—me with my trusty rods, and the rest, as it turned out, with nothing but a couple of poles from the lodge, where fishing was discouraged in favor of bird watching.

I did not realize how serious the equipment problem was going to be until we had landed, and set out on foot along the shore to the sacred spot, every rock of which I remembered from the last time, years before. I got to the place, assembled my rod, and asked the Governor General if he was ready, prepared to give him the honor of first cast.

Ready with what? He had no rod, so I handed him mine, as any loyal courtier would. He flipped a short cast and there was the bow wave, the wallop, the shout of an angler into a big fish. The rest of the story is mercifully short, and I can only say it may account for my coolness toward the entire Schreyer regime at Government House, as a commander-in-chief of the armed forces, and all that.

His Excellency fished until his arms ached, whereupon he handed my rod to a member of his party, one Sandy MacPherson, the man in charge of switching Canada to the metric system. MacPherson had been trying to fish with one of the lodge's old rods, but had not been able to untangle the line sufficiently to get a cast into the water. He accepted my rod from the Gov's hands with a bow, made a cast, and was into a fish.

By the time MacPherson was finished, the pilots announced it was time to head back to Bathurst Inlet, and Governor General Schreyer agreed.

While MacPherson was fishing, His Ex had turned his attention to a pack of Arctic wolves that had approached us from the rear, too close for Governor Generality comfort. He proceeded to peg rocks at them, and the wolves retreated, enabling us to say forevermore that we had been saved by the Governor General's own hand.

MacPherson had the best fishing of his life, and at least I got my rod back for the trip home. I have never really felt comfortable with the metric system ever since.

And, even though Roly Michener had fished the Hugnetuk first, and acquitted himself well with his own gear, my advice is not to go fishing with Governors General, at least not without checking out their equipment. When the government was looking for a farewell gift to Schreyer, I suggested a fishing outfit, and I think they got him one. But I don't know whether he ever used it.

THEY MAY BE CLOSER THAN YOU THINK

Given a choice, nobody ever fishes the home pool, and the wonder is that so many fishing camps were built where the fishing is worst.

Perhaps things were different when the camps were put up, and so what became the home pool was the first to be fished out, leaving the good water as far from camp as bugs and bogs could be endured. Maybe anglers of earlier times believed, as we now must, that you have to suffer to get there.

It may have been that the camps were located for the best scenery, though scenery was not as much a preoccupation then as it is today, as witness all the camps built, like farmhouses, with their backs to the view.

It has been my fate to do more than my share of home pool fishing, and the results would indicate that the reason those waters are so inclined to be unproductive is that they are fished so little. Put a bit of pressure on and the fish are there—or, at least, they may be.

Once at the Maganassippi, I arrived for a week's fishing just as the forests and roads were closed because of the risk of fires. I elected to stay in camp for a week of reading, having pledged that I would not venture outside the building except to go to the outhouse—an outhouse, I might add, with one of the great views of lake and forest, provided you kept the door open, which, being an all-male congregation, we did. Within two days I had cabin fever and ventured down to the dock for a few casts, following which it was a simple matter to untie a rowboat and set out around the lake, dangling a line.

In six days of this furtive fishing, I caught enough trout for supper and had as pleasurable a time as I could remember, heightened by the zest of being a lawbreaker, sharing the joys of the poaching fraternity, along with the taste of fresh trout. Needless to say, my catches were not entered in the club log, itself a violation of the rules, but nobody should be required to testify against himself.

The most dramatic home pool I have ever seen was on the Little Cascapaedia river in the Gaspé, a stream once renowned for its fishing, but now overshadowed by its bigger sister, the Grand Cascapaedia, where the big fish are.

The Little Cascapaedia has yielded salmon up to fifty pounds in its day, and the camps along its banks contain photographs and cutouts to verify the claim. The water in the river is like gin, double-distilled gin, the kind with a slight tinge of purple to it as the light gleams through. The effect of canoeing on the river is magical, because the river bottom is gravel, and the waters never get muddy. They flow over the gravel in such a way that the canoe seems to be gliding, suspended, in the air, and if you keep your eyes down, you can be hypnotized by the colors in the riverbed. But not by the fish. There are fish, we are assured, but you do not see them. What you are more likely to see are swimmers floating downstream in gigantic inner tubes, as many as eight or ten at a time, singing and splashing and shouting and drifting right through what used to be some of the most famous salmon pools in the Gaspé.

No matter—if you really went salmon fishing, and you are lucky, there might be a vacancy for a rod or two on the Grand Caspadaedia, its pools signposted on the highway that runs parallel to the river for almost its full length. It is on that highway that huge flocks of Evening Grosbeaks spend their summers, feeding on the winter salt that is left on the pavement, and being massacred by trucks and cars that speed over the highway, littering the asphalt with dead birds, the crushed yellow-and-black plumage scattered about like banana peels in mourning. I have suggested an annual collection of these vivid feathers, to be used as the basis for a distinctive salmon fly that would bear the region's trademark, but nobody seemed inclined to take it up—perhaps because anglers on the Grand Cascapaedia were too busy with the fish, and those on the Little Cascapaedia had gone elsewhere, or were swimming in the crystal waters.

The main home pool on that river is worth a trip just to look at it, because, when water that clear goes to a depth of three or four meters, the effect is magical—and there, in that water, suspended like carved ornaments in glass, are the salmon.

Ten of them, just idling there with scarcely a movement, heads pointed upstream. They are in line astern, the biggest fish at the front and the smallest ones behind, and you can pass any fly you like over them without the slightest stirring of interest.

We had made two runs on the river without result, when my wife decided, against all advice, to concentrate on the fish in the home pool, and she set to work passing a series of flies over them. It was only after an hour that there was some movement—one of the smaller fish tried to move to the head of the queue and was bunted back by the lead salmon, resuming its place in the rear. That same fish made one more attempt to advance, and again was sent back.

Inspired by this movement, my wife decided to concentrate on that errant salmon, and over it she passed every fly in her book, only occasionally getting a twitch of a fin or a wave of the tail by way of encouragement.

Let Madame tell the rest:

Then I decided to use the Black Bear Green Butt, having killed my first salmon with it on the Vieux Fort (Author's note: *the*

Old Fort to me), that fly having been recommended to me by my husband's son, the judge.

The fly was in the deerstalker hat I was wearing—a double-barbed hook Black Bear Green Butt, specially tied in Montréal, on a Number Eight hook.

The guide laughed at me, and said, "Fish don't take that fly in this river."

And I said, "Well, I trust that fly."

"Anyway," the guide said, "these fish won't take anything. It doesn't matter what fly you cast over them, they just don't want to take. Never have."

And I said, "That little frisky one at the back, he wants to do something. He's bored. And if that big guy would just let him by, he would go right up the river. So I'm going to try him."

The guide shrugged his shoulder, and said, "Suit yourself, you're wasting your time." And then he put the fly on, and I cast just in front of the small salmon.

He darted for it, as it drifted by.

The guide said, "What? What? Do that again! Do it again!"

So I dropped it gently just a little bit ahead of him and to the left, and moved it straight towards him, and sort of twitched it in a V right in front of him, and he went for it. Unlike other times, when I waited to see if a fish was well hooked, I was afraid he would go under the ledge, so I really horsed him as soon as he took, and yanked him.

I could see the whole thing, which is very unusual, because the water was so clear, and so deep. I had noticed he seemed to be always going to his left when he was twitching, so that's where I put the fly, and it worked. It took only a few seconds from the first yank, until I fell to my knees and the fish landed right next to me with a great big plop. You could see the fly was in the side of his mouth, where he had taken it. He was so lively the guide just had time to grab him, before he could slither off the rock back into the water. In a flash he banged him over the head, took the fly out of his mouth, and held him up, crying, "He's a beauty!"

The guide notched his tail so we could distinguish him from the rest of the catch, but there were no more. He was delicious.

OUR NATIONAL RODENT

I have had two cottages in the Gatineau Hills north of Ottawa, one twelve minutes' drive from the capital on Kingsmere, and the other forty-five minutes away on Lac Bernard.

The fishing in Kingsmere used to be good in Mackenzie King's time, and I have a tracing of a five-pound speckled trout taken from its waters by a woman angler in 1942. It used to be a great place to watch the trout spawning in the fall, but in recent years the pressure has cut down on the catch, even for the springtime poachers who arrive when the ice goes out.

It was my habit to use our dock for some practice casts before setting out on serious fishing expeditions. Suffice to say that, on at least two occasions, I caught more trout practicing off that dock than I did in a week of angling in the wilds.

At Lac Bernard, there are no trout, but the lake is well known for its large-mouth bass and pike. Since the lake has a twenty-four-mile shoreline and four hundred cottages, you have to know where the fish are—and where they are, in my experience, is right off my dock.

Perhaps it's just me—I have written about this phenomenon in the papers, as a result of which swarms of boats have descended on us, everybody fishing mightily, but nobody has ever seemed to catch anything.

The first indication of my prowess off the dock came when a nine-year-old granddaughter asked grandda to show her how to fish.

I got out the spinning tackle, and we went to the dock for a few demonstration casts. First cast, a mighty large-mouth bass took hold—leaping, running, doing all the things bass are supposed to do, and bearing out the suspicion that, gram for gram, they outfight the trout.

We brought the fish in, and granddaughter netted it, and then couldn't answer the riddle of whether to keep, or release. The fish weighed a kilo and a half, so it was a weighty decision, and we put it in the well of the paddleboat, which was full of water at the time. After many inspections and long debate, release was decreed.

Then a second granddaughter, age four, appeared and demanded that she catch one, too.

Mealtime intervened, but later, granddaughter number one said she would like another fish.

So we cast again, and again, *wham!*

This time, a pike of some consequence. When it was landed, the matter arose of how to dispatch the fish. There being no other weapon handy, an oar from the rowboat was brought into play.

Now, killing a large pike with an oar is an ugly business, especially when one's granddaughter is holding the fish, and she broke into tears when the blow was struck, showering her with fish goo and other by-products of the kill. She vowed never to speak to me again, much less ever go fishing with me. She quit the game with the idea fixed for life that fishing was a simple, if messy, matter of one cast, one fish, every time.

On a subsequent occasion, I was alone and gave a cast off of the dock, *Boom!* This time, a pike of enormous dimensions, the biggest I had ever seen, and on our lake they run to over ten kilos.

In the middle of the battle, I realized I had left the net in the boathouse behind me, and it was at the back. What to do?

Slowly, I backed along the dock toward the boathouse door, playing the fish. Reaching behind, I slid open the door and backed inside, the rod bent double, the fish fighting fiercely.

All the way to the rear of the boathouse I backed and, feeling behind me, got hold of the net. I then fished my way forward, out of the door, on to the end of the dock, and landed this whopper.

A few days later, a young woman visitor expressed an interest in seeing a fish caught, so it was down to the dock again and, in a single cast, a gorgeous bass leaped, mouthing the Mepps' Black Fury lure that was bringing all this action. This fish jumped four times and was finally netted by the young woman, who decreed immediate release.

"Thank you for showing me what fishing is all about," said she.

I tried to explain, as I had to my granddaughter, that it wasn't about that at all, and that one could fish for days without ever seeing one, and that, in fifty-five years of fishing, I had never encountered anything like this.

To no avail—another fishing career had started and ended in a single cast.

As for myself, I stopped fishing off our dock when the beaver moved in. Beaver in the plural, that is. It started when one showed up and left some chewed twigs behind. Then there were two, and some branches. Then three, and tree trunks. When the count got to seven, the house they were building filled the space below our boathouse and was spilling out into the lake.

I'm not sure what this has to do with the fishing—I have always assumed there might be fish wherever there is a beaver house, and have always paused for at least a few casts, usually at the expense of a fly or a lure or two, because of all the branches they have stored offshore. Quite often, though, there are fish there—either they were there before, or the beaver habitat attracted them.

The beaver is not a fish-eater, so I have always been fonder of Mr. and Mrs. Beaver than of Mr. and Mrs. Loon, who eat an estimated five kilos of fish a day. Loons are smart, and they have energy to burn, but cannot be expected to live on wood, the way beaver do.

As I soon discovered, after the beaver invasion, they use a lot of wood. And not just poplar—big logs of cedar, and birch. As fast as they brought it to their homesite under our boathouse, I tried to shunt it back into the lake, but they kept gaining, physically and intellectually.

Soon they had built our rowboat into their structure, and it looked as though the paddleboat and sailboat would be next. We turned on the boathouse pump, hoping the noise would frighten them off, only to find, the next day, we had no water up at the cottage. The beaver had jammed a piece of wood into the big pulley of the piston pump, stopping it cold. We extracted the stick and tried again, and this time, when the water stopped, it turned out the beaver gnawed out a piece of the plastic pipe leading from the lake to the pump, and built the pipe into the beaver house.

We appealed to the wardens of the nearby park, and they loaned us a Havaheart trap, the kind used to capture small animals alive so they can be transported elsewhere. But we were warned that beaver are much more single-minded than raccoons, and are not inclined to enter any trap they can see, no matter what bait is offered. In our case, we were advised to use carrots and poplar leaves.

We set the thing night after night, and even put some prize sticks from the beaver house beside the trap, knowing they would come back for them, and maybe bite on the carrot wheeze. Come back they did, and the trap door was sprung, but there was no beaver inside, just wrinkled carrots and withered poplar leaves. After several nights of trying, we returned the trap to the wardens.

Trouble was, we developed an admiration for the beaver, even though they weren't being very sporting by appropriating our boathouse as a roof for their dwelling, when everybody knows beaver are supposed to work right out in the open where we can see them.

We pondered: what of the barbecued beaver we could have if we called in the rifle brigade, or a fur trapper? Finally, we abandoned all thoughts of expelling them, and resigned our-selves to life with the beaver family. My wife started worrying whether they would be warm enough in winter.

Our appeals for suggestions brought few replies. One woman came up to me in the local supermarket and said she had the answer: pour diesel fuel on the house. She didn't sug-gest lighting it—just pour on the fuel and the beaver would be repelled by the smell, thus explaining why there are so few beaver at truck stops and bus depots.

We decided we wouldn't like the smell of diesel fuel, ei-ther—in fact, the smell of beaver isn't all that great, when you get right down to it—not so much musky as moldy. (They may, of course, feel the same about us.)

A more constructive approach was taken by a friend, Mr. Colin Haworth of Montréal, a noted guitar player who wrote that we should not count on other folk around the lake helping with the direct method of ripping down the house every morn-ing, because it would be a long, lonely, tough and smelly job.

He went on to say that what you do is wait until late fall, just before the freeze-up, when beaver go cutting crazy and start dropping trees all over the lot.

"The advantage of waiting," he wrote, "is that, at this point, three or four of your neighbours will have had big trees crunch through their roof, or bring down their hydro lines or phone and fax connections.

"This serious loss will bring them to your side, to form an action committee. The committee will then seek out an Indian who has trapping rights, to come quickly and gather some easy legal pelts."

So we waited, meanwhile calling a few trappers in the re-gion, who inspected the setup and said the beaver had made their house impregnable by concealing their "doors" under the boathouse. Besides, the pelts weren't worth anything any more, because furs were unsaleable, no matter that, had it not been for the beaver, there would have been no Canada as we know it.

I consoled myself that, if we had to lose, it could not have been to a finer national symbol, and I was glad Canada hadn't chosen the crocodile, the lion, the elephant or the skunk.

Sure enough, come last fall, the trees started coming down all around our part of the lake. The ice was in when we heard that a neighbor, who shall be unnamed, came by with a rifle and potted seven, with a fine disregard for the beaver's claim to have had the lake first. (Not so—the trappers told me that twenty years ago they never saw one in the Gatineau, and now they are everywhere.) The local record for one beaver house is twelve occupants, one trapper having caught that many out of a single lodge.

If I knew which neighbor it was, I would have asked for a couple of carcasses for the barbecue—the meat tastes like wild goose, as I recall from a couple a trapper gave me. (They had been feeding in a maple forest—how Canadian can you get?)

If our beaver have gone, there remains the question of what to do with four tonnes of wood, weeds and rock-hard mud, constituting one beaver house, projecting far out into the lake and interfering with the fishing off the dock. One ill-disposed neighbor says I am supposed to chop it up and put it in the garbage. Others say I can't float it out into the lake, because it would be a hazard to the speedboats which, come to think of it, isn't such a bad idea.

MADE IN JAPAN

S ome fish are endangered species, and some are extinct. And some never existed at all.

It depends on the evidence, and my evidence is that two extinct species are the ouananiche, or landlocked salmon, of Lac St–Jean, and the muskellonge, everywhere.

In fact, I doubt that the muskies ever occurred anywhere, despite all the evidence that exists on mantlepieces, where lacquered versions of these monsters repose.

My theory about muskies is that there has long been a factory in Japan making them for the North American mantlepiece trade, and that they introduce them into the market in a clever way, with backup stories about how they were caught, how they fought, and the fearsomeness of the breed. The original model for this Japanese sculpture work was the crocodile.

More of this in a moment—let me dispose briefly of the fabled ouananiche of Lac St–Jean. In this case, I do not suggest the fish never really existed—obviously they did, and still do in other waters, other provinces, and I myself have caught one in New Brunswick's Lake Orimocto, through the winter ice.

In Lac St–Jean, a big sporting industry was built around these noble fish, and it still keeps up the pretense that the landlocked salmon are there, although they are not. Days of trolling for them, with guides who remember better days, led to deep frustration, the boredom being broken only by flights of Québec water bombers practicing nearby, scooping up great gulps of lake water and dropping it in clouds with built-in rainbows.

Trolling for ouananiche involves trailing three lines, one on each side of the outboard motor and one right over the top. To each line is affixed a Rapallo minnow lure, each of a different color—and these Finnish lures come in as many colors as salmon flies. The guides grade them according to size and the weather of the day, and once they are in the water, they tickle each line every so often, to see if there is a fish attached.

Should one of the lures take a fish, there is a commotion to identify that lure by size and color, and change the others to match. Not only that, the word is spread to other boats working the territory, and everybody changes.

Under heavy questioning, the guides will admit they are observing a ritual passed down to them by their fathers, who fished when there was action in Lac St–Jean. There is none now, and while there is every reason to explore this charming region of the real Québec, fishing for ouananiche is not one of them.

As to the muskillonge, or maskinonge, or a half-dozen other spellings of this mythical fish, forget it—unless you have one of those Japanese examples left to you by an ancestor. (You can get them new, if you know the right brokers.)

I have dredged for them in the waters where their fame is greatest—the French River, the Bay of Quinté, Rice Lake, and the Rideau and Ottawa rivers. I have heard Greg Clark tell about the giant muskie that jumped into his boat and wound up with Greg's sweater on.

I have seen paintings and photographs of muskies, and read descriptions of the fight they put up, rivalled only by the tarpon.

None of this is convincing.

I have seen, in Bay of Quinté country and environs, barns with what are said to be muskie heads decorating the walls, some as big as mooseheads. Where did I think those came from?

Well, any Japanese factory than can produce a full-size muskie can produce muskie skulls, as well, eh?

In quest of these mythical beasts, I have trolled lures so big they bent my rod double. These are expensive to buy, and expensive to lose, as lose them you must, because the fish are said to live in weeds and reeds that will snag the wiliest hardware and swallow it up.

I have discussed muskies with purported experts, who have devoted, they swear, a life of fishing to the breed, claiming that, once you have hooked one, you will fish for no other on lake or ocean. My esteemed colleague, Douglas Fisher of *The Toronto Sun*, says he spent the summers of his early life as a guide on lakes back of Thunder Bay, helping American anglers land trophy muskies, so many he couldn't remember. There were muskies there, all right. No doubt about it. Hundreds of them. Thousands.

What I think has caused the confusion is the pike, which does abound in Canadian waters, and indeed in waters everywhere, since I have encountered examples of it in Southern France and Northern China, as well as in all the waters I have fished for muskies. The northern pike runs as high as forty pounds, maybe higher in trophy country, and, while it has no great reputation as a fighter, it gives a good pull when it takes.

The degree of fight has something to do with the weight of the tackle, and people don't rig as heavily for the pike as for the muskie, because pike fishermen secretly hope that they will hook a bass. After a day of catching pike and bass they get addled in their minds, and attribute the fighting qualities of the bass to the pike, and the size of the pike to the bass, and out of it all comes the image of the muskie.

Forget it.

Be happy with the pike or the bass, both of which make good eating if they are properly annointed. Do not ever try to eat a muskie, because those Japanese versions are made of a mixture of plaster of Paris, rubber and plastic, and they do not taste good. If you should find one of these in a freezer, do not be fooled—the directions that come with them say to put them there occasionally, for effect.

And, if you wonder how anything could be done so realistically, check out the sailfish and swordfish that anglers bring back from Florida for their walls. These fish exist, and they are caught, and they are taken to stuffing factories to be mounted for northern walls. But what you get back, after payment in the thousands of dollars, is a plastic replica of a fish—it doesn't matter whose. John Diefenbaker had one of those on his wall to the day of his death, and I never had the heart to tell him I'd been in the factory on the Florida Keys, and seen them making those plastic casts by the dozens.

THE BATTLE OF LARRY'S GULCH

The battle of Larry's Gulch went unreported at the time, and indeed the facts about it are still vague, even though I was there at the end and helped clean up the battlefield.

It was the year the government of New Brunswick, Richard Hatfield proprietor, decided it needed some of the province's prized salmon water for itself—ostensibly so it could offer good fishing to people from whom the government wanted favors, chiefly investors who might want to establish plants that would provide jobs in the province.

Almost all the best salmon water was in the hands of rich big-shots, most of them Americans, who bid for the leases at the auctions and managed to keep the best waters to themselves.

My father and his brothers, fishermen all, spent their lives fishing in New Brunswick without once getting a crack at a salmon stream, though they once ventured into Miramichi country and were flattered to be addressed as "sports," when they entered a local grocery store to inquire where they might get some fishing. They got none, having no entrée.

It was Richard Hatfield's inspiration to buy one of the exclusive fishing camps on the best New Brunswick river, the Restigouche, and so it was that Larry's Gulch came to be provincial property, the government taking over the camp buildings, the staff, and the stretch of water that included six salmon pools on a three-kilometer stretch of the river. The acquisition was not widely publicized at the time, nor has it been much written about since—in his novel, *Solomon Gursky Was Here*, Mordecai Richler locates some of his best salmon-fishing bits at Larry's Gulch, which he renamed Vince's, but there is no mistaking the place or its role in the game of power fishing.

Simon Reisman was deputy minister of finance in the federal government, and was honored to head the first group of guests invited to Larry's Gulch after the provincial government takeover. What the New Brunswick government wanted from the federal government was a grant of money to bail out the Bricklin sports-car project—the manufacture of spectacular gullwing-door cars at Minto and Saint John, New Brunswick. The project was plagued with money and technical troubles from the start, though eventually over two thousand cars were produced and are now collectors' items in the exotic-car market. The province dropped over $30,000,000 in the caper, but Hatfield and his government survived, perhaps because of the premier's comment that, "If you're going to take a flier, you might as well take it on something that's fun!" The Bricklin was fun, all right, but among the things wrong with it were that it was a gas guzzler at a time of shortage, that there was uncertainty about what engine it should have, that the gullwing doors leaked (I almost got drowned taking one through a car-wash) and that sale of the car was forbidden in Canada, the cars being for sale in the U.S. only, because of a quirk in the Canada-U.S. auto agreement. Reisman had negotiated that agreement with the United States.

When Reisman got the invitation to fish at Larry's Gulch, he called and invited me along, saying he knew what the New Brunswickers were going to throw at him, and that he had no intention of complying. "But we might get some good fishing," he chortled, "and they'll want to play poker—we should get some money out of *them*!" What really appealed to him was that federal fisheries minister Romeo Leblanc had recently ordered an end to all commercial salmon fishing in New Brunswick waters, ostensibly to save the species, but really to give a shot in the arm to the sports fishery. That meant all nets had been lifted, except those belonging to Indians.

So it was with high hopes that we flew to Fredericton and set out by car up the valley of the St. John, Reisman having asked me to change the subject if our hosts tried to get him into a conversation about the Bricklin.

I had a series of anecdotes up my sleeve, involving Woodstock and Hartland, with its pool and covered bridge, and Perth-Andover, where we stopped for a bite at New Brunswick's most famous (maybe its only famous) restaurant, York's, where every bite is a meal. I regaled the group with the story of my Uncle Harry, who rose to become chief engineer of the federal fisheries department, and was one of the world's leading experts on fishways, those ladders of water that are built to enable fish to get around power dams on rivers.

Harry was no fisherman himself, but he was able to think like a fish, which is why his fishways worked—so much so that, after he retired, he was taken into the employ of the government of Iraq to build fishways on the Tigris and Euphrates rivers, and spent a couple of years in Baghdad living high off the hog.

Harry was a prodigious eater—he was a man of enormous girth, despite which he lived to be ninety-three years old, driving his own car until, at eighty-nine, he totalled his new Lincoln Continental on a Florida highway.

When the big power dam was put in on the Tobique River, where it cascades into the St. John above Perth-Andover, Harry had the job of building what was then the world's highest fish ladder—so high, critics said, there was no way fish could ever be persuaded to climb it.

Harry studied the problem and came up with his own solution. He designed the system and supervised its construction. On the day appointed for filling it with water and testing the hydraulics, Harry was tucking into a gigantic breakfast at York's, his napkin tucked into the neck of his shirt.

An excited group of workers from the dam site burst into the big room and ran up to his table.

"It works!" one of them shouted.

"What works?" asked Harry, between bites.

"The fishway!" was the reply.

Another worker joined in. "We filled it with water and opened the gates, and damned if salmon didn't start coming into it, and they headed up, and they rested in the pools, and they made it all the way to the top. It works! It works!"

"Well," said Harry, taking another bite, "what the hell do you think we built it for?"

"Ya gotta come and see it!"

"See it?" said Harry. "What for? I built it, didn't I?"

And soon thereafter he was headed back for Ottawa, the despair of his brothers, including my father, who couldn't imagine a man having access to some of the world's best fishing and never wetting a line.

The story of Uncle Harry kept us occupied almost to St. Leonard, where we cut off the Trans-Canada Highway northeast through St. Quentin and Kedgwick, into Restigouche country.

It had been a four-hour drive, and for most of it Reisman's hosts tried to get him to talk business, but all he wanted to talk about was fishing, and how they negotiated acquisition of Larry's Gulch, and how much it cost, and all the sorts of things his hosts did not want to discuss, their minds being clouded by thoughts of the Bricklin.

We turned into the road leading to the camp, and when we got near, we were greeted by a long line of parked vehicles—cars, trucks, vans, Jeeps. It was the sort of scene you associated with country auctions or church picnics. When we got close to the camp, there were police cars, and people shouting, and much milling about. There were men, women, and children, and a proliferation of fishing gear that didn't go with the image of the Restigouche as a pristine river where everything but fly fishing was forbidden, and even that was closely regulated.

In the commotion, we didn't know what to do next, but finally one of the Mounties came over to our car and offered an explanation, followed by the manager of the camp, who was sweating profusely and swearing eloquently, offering an apology to the honored guests.

"Goddam poachers been here all day," he grunted.

Poachers?

If that was what they were, there sure were a lot of them—about two hundred in the camp area, with more strung out along the shores of the river, and on the river itself in an assortment of craft from rubber dinghies to high-powered outboards.

As we pieced the story together, the crowd started arriving early in the morning, venturing onto what had hitherto been forbidden territory. They had read a paragraph in the paper, saying that Larry's Gulch had been bought by the province, and had decided that if it belonged to the government, it belonged to them. And by God, they were going to fish it, a privilege denied not only to them but to their fathers and grandfathers. Having poached the river in the dark of night, they were going to fish it in the open.

And so they came, and when the camp staff ordered them off they kept coming. So the police were called, and, by the time they arrived, there were too many people to be manhandled or threatened, so the Riot Act was read and the townspeople of St. Quentin, Kedgwick and points east and west unlimbered their gear and fished through the day.

In the process, they showed the salmon an assortment of hardware not seen in those sanctified waters before or since—spinners, minnows, worms, and maybe even a fly or two, though fly fishing is not a common method among the rural folk of northern New Brunswick, especially when they are fishing for the pot.

Nobody will ever know how many fish were taken that day by the multitude, but it is presumed there were enough to go around and to feed everybody who came, with some left over for sale, as is the custom. We arrived at day's end, and the Mounties were contenting themselves with shouted offers of no charges and no prosecution, if all present would agree not to come back. The deal was struck, and I do not believe the residents of the area ever struck at Larry's Gulch again, however aggressively they have pursued traditional methods of poaching the river, such as pitchforks and nets. Poaching is no more regarded as crime than bootlegging used to be, it was explained to our party. Reisman needed no explanations, and limited himself to wondering (a) whether they had cleaned the river of fish, and (b) when we could get fishing ourselves.

"And talk about the Bricklin," said our hosts.

So far as I know, that day was the one and only time native New Brunswickers got an unrestricted chance at their own salmon fishing, letting loose a century of frustration.

And, as it happened, the battle of Larry's Gulch did not clean the river of salmon. *Au contraire*, as the "poachers" would have put it (the guides on the Restigouche speak only English, at least in the presence of sports), the river was full of fish—more so than any of the guides at the camp could remember, and their memories went back in some cases forty years. There were tales of the great salmon runs back in history, when anglers were few and salmon so plentiful there were no restrictions on the catch (you can read about it in the logbooks, some parties recording as many as 150 salmon per rod).

Despite the mob scene, we had achieved that miracle of the angling world, arriving at just the right time—weather, water level, temperature and salmon run all coming together.

In the morning, we started, after a night of poker in which Reisman did well at the table, but not so well in the business of sleeping, a matter that he has raised with me many times since.

One of the great hazards of any fishing trip is snoring—you can never be sure about your companions, and you are utterly ignorant about yourself, since the snorer, like the skunk, is unaware of giving offence. I had never believed stories about my own prowess, though friend Bruce West once said he had seldom heard higher decibels, and threatened to use the ultimate treatment on me—a sharp blow to the chops, delivered with the side of the open hand, guaranteed either to check the snorer or kill him.

Throughout the night, Reisman kept shaking me awake and saying: "Stop doing that!"

Since a snorer doesn't know what he (or she) is doing, it is not a very meaningful demand, and seldom yields the desired result.

After several exchanges, I lay awake, fearful of sleep, but the sound of rain on the tin roof of the cabin finally got to me and I drifted off with, as Reisman later put it, all the subtlety of a chain saw hitting a knot. I woke to a flurry of curses and saw Reisman lighting a cigar, sweeping his bedding into his arms and heading out the door and across to the main lodge, growling that he didn't have to put up with this. He slept on a sofa in front of the fireplace and arose, he said, refreshed.

After breakfast we set out on the river, for the best three days of fishing imaginable. If the size of the catch had been an indicator of the federal government's grant for the Bricklin project, they would be making the cars to this day. As it was, Reisman concentrated on the fishing, and so did we all, except our hosts, who kept wanting to change the subject.

Fishing the Restigouche is a special thing, and even when the fish are rising it can be troublesome for anglers who prefer variety in their sport, and who like to wade rather than ride. Restigouche fishing has an element of engineering in it. To begin with, the canoes (first designed and built in Fredericton by my uncle-in-law Will Chestnut) are huge, designed to provide a solid platform for a standing angler.

The guide stations the canoe at the head of the pool, and you fish in a series of drops—casting in an ever-widening downstream arc until every bit of reachable water has been covered, whereupon the anchor is raised momentarily, the canoe slips down a length, and the entire process is repeated, as thoroughly as vacuuming a rug or painting a floor.

Without fish, it can be tedious.

With them, the whole thing takes fire and boredom ceases with a bang. Having seen the salmon at its first jump—the most breathtaking moment in sport except, perhaps, for Ben Johnson's steroid-propelled run in the hundred-meters at the Seoul Olympics—the guide makes the decision of whether or not to put the sport ashore. If the answer is yes, the outboard starts with a roar and ashore you go, on a gravel beach that becomes your running track, because those salmon have speed and, if you are well down on the backing, you had better run, too.

The first salmon that morning left me puffing, and the guide said that would be all for this run—we should go back to camp and rest for the evening fishing. I wanted to continue, but he pointed out that the limit for a day was two, and that, if I caught another one we would be finished until tomorrow. So back we went, soon to be joined by the other anglers, each with his morning's fish.

That evening it was the same—everybody came back with salmon number two. And the next day, morning and evening, the same—everybody "limited out."

The final day I got my first fish early, and the second one late. The second one was the one you remember always (there is usually one such fish every trip), and it came late, just as dusk was falling and it seemed we would return to camp for the last time, empty-handed. But the guide saw a swirl near my fly—I saw nothing—and asked me to reel in, whereupon he put on a huge Black Wulff dry fly, saying, "He'll want that!" He spit on the fly and tossed it into the river, pointing to the spot where the fish was. The first cast had him, and we could almost feel the splash from that opening leap.

I was ashore before I knew it, and feeling a strain on the line unlike the earlier fish.

"A beauty!" said my companion. "He'll go twenty-five pounds."

Darkness fell before I could get the upper hand on the fish, and still he was running and jumping, far out in the river. The guide had a flashlight to light my way as I lumbered up and down the rocky shore, and finally the salmon was close enough for a pass with the net. Flashlight in one hand, and the big net in the other, the guide abandoned all thought of scooping the fish and settled for bringing the net down on top of him. Giving it a mighty twist, he enveloped the fish and brought it ashore, the handle of the net bending.

We made our way back to camp, where the others had been worried about our whereabouts in the dark. Entering the circle of light in front of the main lodge, the guide gave me the salmon to carry, and Reisman says he never saw such a vision of happiness, even though his joy was tempered by the thought that I had caught the biggest fish of the trip.

It went twenty-six pounds—no record-breaker, to be sure, but to this day the biggest salmon I have ever landed.

I brought it home and froze it, and served it as the center-piece at the wedding dinner of my daughter, Lucinda. The chefs at the Rideau Club did a special job on the fish, and it came on a silver platter, garlanded with flowers and herbs. It was set up near the bar, outside the tent where the reception was being held, and while the guests were listening to the toasts, the hired bartenders descended on the salmon and ate most of it.

Few of the guests got any, and I got none. Only fitting, it was agreed, for the father of the bride.

THE JOYS
OF SMOKING

The link between smoking and fishing was pleasure.

It was quiet and contemplative, best when there was no wind and the smoke could curl around your face and you could imagine, as you breathed some of it in through your nose, that it was keeping the bugs away.

Pipe and cigars were best—cigarettes were too quick, and when you flicked the butts into the water they would sometimes bring a trout to the rise, which was frustrating if the fish were ignoring your most delicate casts.

Even in the wind the pipe was good—there were even pipes, put out by fishing-tackle firms, with swivel covers on the bowl to protect the burning tobacco from the breeze, and keep it from smoking too hot.

It was a fact that a pipe smoked in town, at home, or in the car or at the office, would yield only one satisfying smoke in four, and some days none at all, even though you had gone through a whole pouch of tobacco. On stream or lake, the satisfaction was there every time, whether the fishing was good or bad, the weather fair or foul. If it was raining, you could turn the pipe upside down and it still tasted sweet, whether there was sugar-cane brandy to go with it or not.

Between spells of casting, if there was nothing doing, the business of knocking out the bowl and finding the pouch and filling up and bringing out the wooden matches, lighting up and hearing the hiss as the burnt match hit the water, these were all useful and pleasant things to do, even before you took the first deep draw and commenced casting again.

In car or boat, there was no sound quite as ominous as the crack from the hip pocket and the gentle-felt snap of what could only be a broken pipe stem—followed by the mental inventory of your tackle box in the hope of finding tape. Bandaids would do, so would Scotch, or adhesive tape, but the stuff we used to call electric tape was best—the kind that used to give a blue glow when you unwound it.

The trick was to get the pipe back together tightly enough that it would draw—the slightest lack of air could be as aggravating as a cigar with a cracked wrapper—no amount of sucking would make it work.

I remember breaking a pipe at the start of a day's fishing, and the guide, who was portaging our canoe, laid it down on the pine needles (wall to wall on the trail, for this was a camp for rich American newspaper publishers) and stripped a length of black tape off the thwart, where he had wrapped it to ease the load on his shoulders. He mended my pipe, and when I tested it, it was sweet, whereupon companion Bruce West rhapsodized, "Greater love than this no man hath, than that he would give the tape off his thwart!"

If the flies were fierce, you could still smoke a pipe through the netting of a beekeeper's hat, though it could get stuffy in there and the smoke could make your eyes run, especially since the net had already cut vision so it was hard to follow the flight of line and fly. In such circumstances, cigarettes and cigars were out.

Indeed, the cigar required special circumstances for full enjoyment, and lucky was the angler with a few stogies stashed in the tacklebag, or a pocket of the vest or waders, for the time when, full of a good morning's or afternoon's fishing, you could sit back in boat or on streambank and light up, not caring whether it was an expensive one or something bought at the general store on the way in. Like the pipe, there were no bad cigars on the water, and women anglers who had never smoked in their lives were known to share a cigar's delight, and rekindle it on good nights in the tub, with cognac and foam.

High among things of beauty are suspension bridges and sailing ships, Bugatti cars and autumn hardwoods, and some human activities like Karen Kain dancing, or Joe Montana throwing, or Katerina Witt skating. Add to that an angler casting over darkened waters, and for embellishment a waft of pipe smoke and, if only in imagination, a fish rising to take the fly in the air, commencing the fight in a cloud of spray.

Occasionally photographs will catch the magic, and fishing catalogues are full of them, along with videos that show how it is done—but it is best to be there with someone who can cast so pretty a line you pause to watch, and marvel that it is being done without the angler thinking about it. The angler is thinking fish. When fishing, one thinks of little else, while being aware of forest and sky and birds and, on special days, moose or deer or otter, even mink.

Now that smokeless fishing is in fashion, those of us who remember the joys of the bowl are hard put to know what to do with our hands in idle moments. I still reach instinctively for the pouch, and wonder if the matches are dry, and yearn for a particularly sweet-smoking briar that hasn't known a match for eight years, three months, two weeks and four days, and reposes, dank and stale, in a desk drawer at home. I would give it away, but I don't know anybody who smokes anymore, and besides, nobody ever enjoyed smoking somebody else's pipe, anyway.

DREAM RIVER

The Old Fort River is not easy to find on most maps, and even when you get there, you have to be shown where it is, and the guides have to tow the boat through channels in the tall weeds, like Humphrey Bogart pulling the *African Queen*.

The Old Fort is a wilderness river, a throwback to the kind of streams the anglers of the nineteenth century wrote about, with their voracious wild trout and teeming salmon, and stunted trees so slow-growing that what looks like a sapling might be fifty years old. The wood of the spruce is so dense that it weighs as much as oak, and the trees grow only a fraction of the way up the surrounding hills, which are as bare as the northern tundra.

The village of Old Fort, or Vieux Fort in the language that few of the locals speak, consists of houses scattered at random on the rocky shore of Old Fort Bay, on the north shore of the Gulf of St. Lawrence. The local industry is fishing—three months on the water, nine months on Unemployment Insurance. The fanciest house in town is occupied by a family of father, mother and seven sons, all the men registered fishermen, all qualified for the pogey in the off-season, adding $75,000 a year to the family income.

Into this setting, for six weeks of every summer, pour the sports from the United States, looking for the action and finding it. In twenty years, there were only two parties of Canadian fishermen—ours, and four men from Montréal who drank night and day for the full seven days in camp, never leaving the premises. They paid their bill and said they had a good time, though proprietor Sam Fequet wondered what they did that they couldn't have done in their own back yards.

The American parties come to fish, lugging big freezer chests in with them, empty, and taking them out full. Sam Fequet calls his camp Morgain's, either unaware or uncaring that he picked the name of the evil one in the Arthurian legend. He said he just liked the sound of it.

Like American anglers everywhere, the ones who come to the Old Fort carry beautiful equipment, the kind that makes the guides' eyes bulge, even though they are used to seeing the best. Nothing like the fishing platforms the Yanks bring to Canada's more accessible waters, the boats laden with electronic gear, chromed rod-holders and as many automatic gadgets as those Russian factory ships that vacuum the fish out of our offshore waters. But ever since the U.S.A. took over from Britain as the main source of fine rods and tackle for fly fishing, the Americans have set the pace, and most of them know what they are about, as the guides will tell you. They tip well, too—if it were not for sports from the U.S.A., Canadian outfitters would have a thin time of it, because Canadian anglers are not great tippers and, indeed, do not like having to pay for their fishing at all.

My favorite American at the Old Fort had one eye and one leg and he was fat—the last person in the world fitted for a sport involving keen eyesight and sure-footedness on slippery rocks and soggy trails. In fact, he could only fish one pool, accessible by boat and with a solid rocky shore, providing a firm footing. The pool is called Number One, and it is at the head of a long rapid flowing down to Pool Number Two, a fifteen-minute walk below on the riverside trail.

This one-eyed, one-legged, fat fisherman hooked into a salmon that headed downstream, which, most of the time, means that the fish is going to be lost, even if the angler gives pursuit through the foaming waters. Usually, a salmon headed downstream can outpace any pursuer, unless there is a sandy shore along which the angler can run.

In this case, there was no shore, and the angler couldn't run anyway, having only one leg. So, keeping his rod up, the one-legged, one-eyed, fat American headed down through the rapids, bouncing on his bottom like the driver of a runaway horse. He kept a tight line on the fish until the last minute, when the salmon reached Number Two Pool and the angler was still riding the rapids, uttering wild whoops, not of distress, but of joy. When he reached the calmer water he reeled in as fast as he could, but the line had wrapped itself around a rock and, with a final leap, the salmon was free and gone.

The hardest part, as the drenched fisherman put it to me, was getting back up the trail, soaking wet and chilled to the bone. "But it was," he chuckled, "the experience of a lifetime, worth the trip all by itself." He had a dozen salmon in his freezer chest, but the only one he talked about was the one that got away.

For him, as for all who go to the Old Fort, happiness is just thinking about the place, and merely getting there is more than half the fun. Most anglers have a place like that in their heads, or perhaps only in their dreams—like sex, it may be largely in the mind. Unlike sex, it is not diminished if you have to pay for it.

One trip, on our way to the Old Fort we were held up for a day in Deer Lake, Newfoundland, a town on the Humber River, which yields as many salmon to fly fishers in a season as all the other rivers in Eastern Canada put together. But the Humber is Big Water, and we were headed for a smaller river where the fishing was more intense, and where we would be by ourselves.

Trying to figure what to do with the "lost" day, we fell into the company of local anglers Bonner Pinsent, John Andrews and Grant Bagnell, who told us to be in the parking lot of the motel in half an hour, with our waders on and our rods rigged for fishing.

The sight of four sports in full gear in a dry-land parking lot drew some snide comments from passers-by, and I was reminded of a sight I once encountered in the main lobby of Gatwick Airport, outside London. A man was sitting on a stool with a fly rod in his hand, casting over the heads of the milling throng. "Catching much?" I shouted. "You're the tenth today!" came the reply.

I had that answer ready, should there be shouted taunts, but there were none, and soon all sounds were drowned out by the drumming of a helicopter settling on the pavement, its occupants beckoning us aboard. It was explained to us that the helicopter business hasn't been the same since Frank Moores was the premier, it being Moores's custom to keep the choppers busy flying him and his guests to assorted fishing holes around the province.

Off we went, and in fifteen minutes we are at a choice spot on the Humber, with a day's fishing in prospect.

The leader of our party was John Woods, whose family was famed in the sporting world for making high-class camping equipment, and for the invention of the eiderdown sleeping bag, which caused Ernest Hemingway, on a cold outdoor night, to say, "Thank God for the Woods brothers." Hemingway subsequently enshrined the Woods's invention by putting the big love scene in For *Whom the Bell Tolls* in a Woods sleeping bag, immortalized in film by Gary Cooper and Ingrid Bergman.

Woods caught the only salmon on that day on the Humber, and we flew it back to the motel and dined sumptuously on it that night. John also made history of a sort by losing his footing on an outcropping known as Hosscock Rock, so named because of its resemblance to a horse's protuberance. He slid down the rock onto a plateau known as Crooked Reef, and we thought he was done for, since he was too far away for us to help him. He walked kind of funny for the rest of the day and, when he got back to the hotel, he had a hot bath and said he felt better than ever. But ever since, given the slightest encouragement, he tells the story of his fall at Hosscock—like a friend of mine who once fell into the reflecting pool at the Taj Mahal in India, the pool being empty of water at the time. He broke his arm, and never stopped talking about his fall at the Taj Mahal.

The thing about John Woods is that he is a fashion plate, on land or on the water. Nobody dresses better, and when he shows up at the airport for a fishing trip, he is right out of what used to be the Woods Brothers catalogue, now L.L. Bean or Eddie Bauer.

My own dress on such occasions is never up to snuff, and the one time I appeared in a jacket that I thought was smart, John looked at me and sniffed, saying he had designed it himself for the old firm, "for shooting." The implication was that only an idiot would wear a shooting jacket on a fishing trip, but he didn't labor the point.

John Woods's only fall from sartorial elegance was the time he was fishing with his favorite Old Fort guide, Ashley Fequet, and Ashley had been telling him about an old Indian trail he had heard about, on the other side of the river from the trail the sports were using.

Ashley talked about his trail with such emotion that John asked to be shown where it started, at the end of a day's fishing when we were heading back to camp.

Ashley put John ashore at what he said was the starting point, and said we would see him at the top in twenty minutes.

We took the regular trail, and waited for John to emerge.

An hour passed, and no John.

Fifteen minutes more, and still no John.

Half an hour, and there emerged from the bush an apparition that bore no resemblance to the Abercrombie & Fitch man who had started up the trail. His clothes were all askew and torn, his face flushed, and he was spitting flies from a cloud of mosquitoes that almost hid his face from view. The language that was emerging was heavy cussing, even for a fishing trip, and Ashley Fequet was seen to cross himself in mock horror.

"Whistling Jesus!" said John, using an expression once favored by my old father, who heard it from an Acadian construction worker in Moncton, New Brunswick. "You call that a trail? When in hell did the last Indian ever use it?"

"Oh," said Ashley, "I suppose about two hundred years ago. Ain't been any Indians around here since then."

It was after that adventure that Woods agreed to wear a shoo-bug jacket which, while it makes the wearer look like a walking pile of fishnet, keeps the flies at bay, provided you soak it nightly in bug repellent, preferably the Muskol that put Truro, Nova Scotia, on the map. But John always managed to keep his hair combed, and he had the most beguiling habit of rolling his eyes heavenward, which made him look for all the world like Jack Nicholson. Indeed, one time in Los Angeles, he was mistaken for the celebrated actor and obliged a milling crowd by signing autographs, until they found he was signing his own name and turned away, obviously never having looked at the labels on eiderdown sleeping bags which, in any case, are not used in California except in movies about Spain.

One day you could be skunked on the Old Fort, and the next day, in that very same pool, I landed three salmon and lost three more in the space of an hour and a half.

Currie Fequet, who could imitate the calls of the loon to perfection (there are at least six), was also the champion caster of the river, able to get his line out so far the fly and the line itself were lost to sight in the mist. During one demonstration, he had the line snapping like an elongated whip and the fly snapped off from the force, something that was hard to forgive, since it was the hot fly of the trip and I had no more.

The hot flies varied from year to year—stone flies one year, Black Bear Green Butt another, Muddlers a third. Like generals fighting wars, we were always equipped for last year's fishing, and the fly that worked then seldom worked again. Until, that is, we imported the Green Machine from the Miramichi, an innocuous-looking Buck Bug made of deer hair, which seemed to work as well on Old Fort salmon as on the New Brunswick variety.

The Green Machine is a miniaturized version of the lure called the Bomber. I call it a lure because, by no stretch, could it be likened to a fly. What it is, is a cigar butt with spines on it, the sort of thing honest fly fishers would not have considered short years ago, though they smoked plenty of stogies to keep the bugs off, and the expression was that "a woman is only a woman, but a good cigar is a smoke!"

You don't hear that sort of thing much any more, even on fishing trips, and I am reminded of something once written by

Melvin Hueston of Edmonton, in his prize-winning book, *The Great Canadian Lover*, where he warned city anglers about the perils of breathing too much ozone in the outdoors, and recommended filtering it through a wet cigar butt.

(It was Hueston who explained why it is that a trout will take a fly that resembles nothing ever seen in nature. "There are five and a half million species of insect," he wrote, "and a trout, having a brain the size of a BB, cannot be expected to remember them all.")

Which brings me to the biggest salmon ever seen on the Old Fort, a monster that was lurking in the Upper Pool, the prettiest pool of all, where the river starts its run from the chain of lakes above.

Only one of our party believed in the existence of this mighty fish—Earl Clements, a New Brunswicker whose long years of angling on the Miramichi had given him the power to cast like an angel and think like a fish.

On the Old Fort, it is the custom for the guides to look the pool over on arrival and count the number of fish present, sometimes scaling trees in their waders for a better view. Earl deplored this custom, preferring to sneak up on them, saying that, while the guides were counting the salmon in the pool, the salmon were counting the guides and getting spooked in the process.

This day on the top pool, the guides were invited to hang back, and Earl tied on a device that looked like a giant woolly worm, though known in the fishing fraternity as a Giant Bomber.

With his back against the alder bushes, he flicked this object out onto the pool, while the guides shook their heads at the folly of floating such a ragged piece of junk upon the sacred waters.

The guides had dozed off on the shore, as was their custom, by the time Earl had made his sixth cast, whereupon the Biggest Salmon rose from the waters—or, "he riz," in the local lingo—to what seemed like treetop height (the trees are stunted there), and fell back with a splash, the cigar butt firmly fixed in his mouth.

The sound of the watery explosion echoed up the lake and down the river, awakening the guides and causing them to exclaim, when the fish jumped again, that they had never beheld such a sight in their lives, may they be struck dead in their tracks if they had.

Our angler opined it was a bit early to talk about being struck dead, since the fish was not yet landed, and only he knew that his leader material at the end of his line was three years old, and that last year he had spilled a bottle of fly dope on it, without bothering to wipe it off. Fly dope, as every outdoorsperson knows, can eat its way through stainless steel, and plastic can rot so fast that a person's spectacles can be left with only the lenses, the frames having turned to mush.

Earl kept the knowledge of impending disaster to himself, wishing heartily that, having spent his life's savings to get to the Old Fort, he had blown an additional seventy-nine cents for a new piece of monofilament leader.

Two more jumps and one long run, and it was over—the old nylon, weakened by time and insect repellent, parted, and the monster made off up the lake with the cigar butt bomber still fixed in his face.

Earl was philosophical, saying there were more where that came from, meaning salmon. We worked Earl over pretty good, but he had revenge of a sort when it turned out that the new monofilament we had bought at Ottawa's leading sporting-goods emporium was no better than Earl's old stuff, and must have been on the shelf since Diefenbaker's day. We lost at least six fish to rotten line in the course of the week, which put quite a strain on our philosophy that the scenery was reward enough.

The guides, like guides everywhere, don't talk much, even when spoken to, and it is a characteristic of the people of Old Fort that most of them speak with a stutter. They are Quebeckers but they don't speak French—most of this coastline is inhabited by English-speakers, who, in their lifestyle and way of speaking, can hardly be distinguished form the outport people of Newfoundland. They like to tell you that the first Europeans in these parts were the Vikings. They watch Newfoundland TV, and it is through Newfoundland that they market much of the fresh and salt cod that supplements their income from unemployment insurance. When they want to drive to Québec proper, they have to go through Newfoundland, Nova Scotia and New Brunswick to get there, a trip of at least three days. Building a coastal road westward to hook up with the Québec highway system would cost too much, because so many rivers would have to be bridged—great salmon rivers, most of them, still great because they are so hard to get to.

Old Fort Village has fifty-five families, half of them named Fequet, and the rest Wellmans and Greens and Dredges and Buckles, all Anglicans, 350 souls in all, consuming 8,500 cases of beer in an average winter.

I first heard of this part of the world as an angling paradise almost forty years ago, in Richmond, Virginia. Working for Reuters News Agency, I was making my way through the Southern states, trying to interest newspapers there in taking our service, and I had an appointment in Richmond to see the local newspaper tycoon, John Dana Wise. It turned out he wasn't much interested in talking about our news service, much less taking it, though he was the soul of hospitality, giving rise to that joke among carpetbagger salesmen in the South—"I'll drink your mint juleps, but don't give me any of that goddam hospitality," meaning that it is no good being killed with courtesy, when it's no sale.

Mr. Wise, the moment he heard I was from Canada, launched into the most rhapsodic description of his annual pilgrimages to Newfoundland for the salmon, on the River of Ponds. I have since seen that river and have a hard time matching it to his description, but I can hear him yet, in melodious accents, describing the taking of salmon, and the tailing of them (landing them without a net), releasing them ever so gently back into the stream. All of this was interspersed with incredulity that I, a Canadian, had not known such joys, and he wished me the chance to try for salmon in later life, a wish copiously granted. I remember John Dana Wise for that, and for a horrific warning he gave me when we parted, my order book empty. "Look out for the ticks," he said. "One hot afternoon, I was lying in my bunk buck naked and I fell asleep, and one of those scoundrels dropped off the ceiling and landed right on my peter and dug himself in there. I had such a swelling they had to take me to the hospital, and it was weeks before I was comfortable from what that critter did to me."

That tale of the tick has remained with me as vividly as the warning my Uncle Frank once gave to my cousin Dave when we went fishing for trout on Loch Lomond, outside our home town of Saint John, New Brunswick.

It had been raining during the night and, when we got our hired rowboat, the seats were wet. Cousin Dave sat on the wet seat, and Uncle Frank frowned and growled, "Don't sit on a wet seat, lad!"

"Why, uncle?"

"Because you'll get piles, that's why."

"What are piles?"

A long pause. Then, "Well, imagine there's a bale of barbed wire, and they build a big fire and they put the bale of wire in until it gets white-hot."

"Then what?"

"Well, they pull the hot barbed wire out of the fire and they stuff it up your behind very carefully, so you don't feel anything until it's all in there."

Cousin Dave was squirming by now, as was I, waiting for the punch line.

"And then," said Uncle Frank, his eyes bulging, "they *PULL* it!"

Neither Cousin Dave nor I have ever sat on a wet seat since then, nor have I fallen asleep stark in tick country, thanks be to Uncle Frank and John Dana Wise, both now long gone.

Newfoundlanders you meet on fishing trips are not just honest, they are kind, especially to strangers. They are perhaps the last people in Canada to go out of their way to help tourists, a species regarded with increasing supicion just about everywhere else in the country, especially in Ottawa, where the annual appeal to be polite to tourists is the subject of protest demonstrations on Parliament Hill.

We have had Newfoundland merchants open their stores for us after hours, and bootleggers come up with bottles of overproof rum (not that awful Screech), and even airlines have put themselves out to accommodate us. Fishermen have shown us the way to their favorite holes, and waitresses have brought us extra helpings of cod tongues because "the first plate was so small."

I doubt that Newfoundlanders treat one another as well as they treat outsiders in their midst, but I am sure they would return a man's lost gear with the same honesty the Chinese used to show in Chairman Mao's time, when they would pursue you if you left behind a folder of matches.

I mention this because, on the return from one fishing trip to The Labrador (it was really the Old Fort in Québec, but we always called it part of The Labrador, and you can see why on the map, even though the boundaries are in deep dispute.), I lost the suitcase with all my fishing gear. It bounced off the top of the car coming in from the airport, and was never returned, though bits and pieces of my stuff were found in a trashcan near the airport.

Gone were the chest waders that had sustained me through all the days of salmon fishing, and whose weight I cursed during the tramps over trails deep in muck. These things were the precursors of pantyhose, but they weighed a lot more and had a nice pouch in the front, where you could carry pipe tobacco and a flask, and stuff in the occasional trout.

Gone was the fishing vest and all the little pockets for the assorted aids to fishing, like fly dope, spare leaders, boxes of flies, pocket knives, waterproof matches and tranquilizers. (Yes, waterproof matches, from Australia, that would light soaking wet—no need to wrap in condoms.)

Gone, the moleskin britches made by the Cambrian Flyfishers of Wales, which were to have lasted me a lifetime and were useful, not only as fishing pants, but for cross-country skiing as well. They were bought for me at Farlow's in London—those doughty rivals of Hardy's Angling on Pall Mall, and some say the best—and I was just getting them broken in.

Gone, my Eddie Bauer buckskin shirt, comfortable in heat or cold, and proof against the probing beaks of the fiercest northern mosquitoes, though a nest of blackflies once got up the sleeve and gnawed me raw.

Gone, the Gore-Tex raingear, guaranteed to breathe, while keeping the wet out at the same time, which is like being able to rub your tummy and pat your head while chewing gum. It wouldn't, of course, but it did help break the wind on long cold boat rides.

Gone, a dozen pairs of dirty underwear and socks, there being no place to do laundry at the Old Fort, any more than we dared to try the Rube Goldberg shower provided by the proprietor for fastidious Yanks, consisting of a sump pump in the lake and a hose leading to an oil drum slung up in a tree.

The risk of being marooned goes with every airborne venture into the Canadian bush, but having flown to Old Fort three times previously without incident or delay, we had been lulled into a false sense of security.

An extra day in camp wouldn't matter, if you could fish. But you can't, because the waters are deemed to belong to the incoming party. Two extra days in camp without fishing and things begin to get serious. A condensed-milk sandwich may be okay as a noonday lunch beside a salmon pool, but in camp it is horrible, even if the cook adds chocolate and calls it a fudge sandwich. (These concoctions have as their base a tin of condensed milk, put in boiling water for forty-five minutes, after which it turns to pudding and can be used in various ways, including the filling in a sandwich. The fact that the bread is fresh-baked helps.)

Three extra days in camp and members of the party begin eyeing one another with thoughts of cannibalism. No matter how close the anglers may be, how fond of one another, there is only so much conversation when the circumstances are forced, and sullen silence sets in, made deeper by the fact that everybody is listening for the sound of a floatplane. Dwelling on how miserable the incoming Yanks must be, cooling their waders in Deer Lake, cease to comfort.

The younger members of our party broke into dissent and wailings, spiced by outhouse humor. When this kind of thing palled, we concentrated on the path to the camp outhouse—the little shack with the sign inside saying that ladies must remain seated throughout the performance. The female member of our party, another year, laughed at that and said no woman had ever been known to sit on a public toilet seat. They squat.

What was charming about the outhouse trail was that it was carpeted with spruce needles and could be walked without danger of sinking to your waist in muck. On the outhouse trail there were three broods of grouse, the young ones so tame they could be picked up by hand, and the parents so dumb the guide said they could walk right up to them and wring their necks. We voted against this, despite visions of how good a grouse dinner would be, in place of those sandwiches.

We did think of having a Merganser shoot, but the proprietor said it was against the law, much as he would like to thin out the population of that pretty but pesky duck, devourer of more fish than any anglers would account for in a decade. Shooting Mergansers used to be standard practice on salmon rivers—some of the mother birds swim with as many as twenty ducklings behind them, and it is a thrill to see them going upstream against heavy rapids, and even waterfalls. That they hurt the fishing there is no doubt—after the Mergansers have swum through a pool there is no point in fishing for at least an hour, because even the big salmon will lie low, seeming to remember the menace from their youth. The bigger fish have nothing to fear from the Mergansers, but they do from the Osprey, and the Old Fort has one giant nest right over the Number Two Pool, from which we could watch these great birds do their aerobatics.

On Day Four of our vigil, we decided to set out on foot for the village, carrying with us the salmon Sam had smoked, and hopeful of a lift along the coast to Blanc Sablon, where the ferry runs across the Strait of Belle Isle to Newfoundland. From where we were, Blanc Sablon sounded like Gay Parée—there had to be something there because it's where Brigitte Bardot parked her parka when she came to fight the sealers and, as it turned out, put the boots to the very fur industry that opened up the North American continent to white settlement. (Newfoundlanders use the word white without apology, because they have no natives to answer to—the original European intruders killed every last one.)

We had just started our walk out of Old Fort Village when, suddenly, two floatplanes appeared out of the fog, landed in the bay and poked their pontoons onto the rocky shore, so we could leap aboard through the surf. They had dropped the incoming Yanks at the camp and set off to find us. We divided our party of five between the two Beavers (the plural of beaver, the animal, is beaver, but Beaver, the aircraft, is Beavers) and there followed a sunset flight across the Gulf and down the west coast of Newfoundland. We were operating on Montréal time, which, by Québec law, prevails to the easternmost tip of *La Belle Province*, where it looks across at Newfoundland, where the time is an hour and half later. On the Québec shore, this means the midsummer sun rises before 4:00 a.m. and sets around 6:00, a device thought to be designed to get the anglers in off the pools in time for an early dinner.

The upshot was that the last part of our flight was in the dark, through the mountains of Gros Morne National Park, winding up with a landing on the water of the Humber River, in a place that was filled with pulpwood. The pilot explained to me that it was going to be a bit tricky, and I asked him why he didn't turn on the landing lights. He said it was because he could see better in the dark. It worked, and within an hour we were all taking hot baths, prior to sitting at separate tables for a midnight repast.

There is a way to get to The Labrador by road and ferry, but you soon run out of road on the other side. Happily, the part of the road that is in Québec runs as far as Old Fort, which, for fishing purposes, is just far enough.

The drive up the west coast of Newfoundland runs through Gros Morne National Park, which is reason enough for going there, and you cross a lot of salmon rivers on the way, including the greatest of them all, the Humber, and further north, the River of Ponds, mentioned earlier in this chronicle.

The ferry for Labrador leaves from St. Barbe, a one-time Newfoundland outport and now a thriving fishing and tourist town, where they have hard porn on the TV at Doyle's Motel, which accounts for the glazed looks on the faces of the truck drivers who frequent the place. Their big rigs provide most of the business on the ferry and on the highway known as The Viking Trail, because it leads north to l'Anse aux Meadows, where the Norsemen made their first westerly landfall a thousand years ago.

What the locals call "the friggin' ferry" runs across the Strait of Belle Isle to Blanc Sablon, from where it is an eighty-kilometer drive to Old Fort. The first time we drove it, the road was a one-lane dirt track, but it has gradually been widened and paved and is not bad, if you like rocks for scenery—the kind of stuff that won The Labrador the title of "the land God gave Cain." To make up for it, there is the fishing.

One trip on the ferry, we were delayed because one of the big rigs got jammed in the entrance door to the ship, and they had to let the air out of eighteen tires to get it aboard, and get it off at Blanc Sablon. Turned out they didn't have any free air in Blanc Sablon, and the driver was last seen starting the job of pumping up all those tires by hand.

We had our own problems that trip, because a construction crew was rebuilding the bridge across the West Brador River, and they said it would take three days. For us, those were bought-and-paid-for days on the Old Fort, and when after salmon, the important thing is to let nothing get in your way. We walked across the naked girders of the bridge, trying to ignore the torrent below, and managed to hitch-hike our way to Old Fort, thanks to the kindness of drivers who were marooned on the other side of the bridge.

That was the year of the fly known as the Black Bear Green Butt, the only thing the salmon seemed interested in. Every year it was a different favorite—the Green Machine, the Silver Rat, the Rat Face MacDougall, the White Wuff, and the one fly that originated on the Old Fort, the Roger's Fancy. That one was tied by arch-angler Shirley Woods for his friend, General Roger Rowley, on their first trip to the Old Fort, Rowley having expressed the hunch that the salmon that year were looking for something green. The pattern worked and has gone into international usage.

The year of the Black Bear Green Butt, it turned out we had only three of them among the four of us, and by Day Four they were gone, so much mourned that the next year we brought two dozen, and they didn't take a fish—I still have a surplus of them in my box.

That was the last year I wore heavy rubber chest waders, before discovering the lightweight models that have revolutionized, not only angling, but the equally important sport of trail trudging. I learned the Old Fort remedy for leaky waders—you cut the toes off them and the water runs out! Before making that discovery, I learned something else—when your waders are full of cold water, do not sit down and put your feet up. The howls, as the icy water rushed up into my vitals, echoed through the hills, rivalling the wildest cries of the loon.

There is a lot to be said about chest waders, and in a lifetime of wearing them, I guess I have said most of it. If you have a lot of walking to do, and what angler does not, you wind up feeling like a medieval knight in armor who has lost his horse and has to get to the joust on foot, with no way to have a relieving pee. (The business of answering nature's call need not be gone into here, except to say that with all the inconvenience of chest waders, men have an easier time of it in the bush than women do, except that the crouch needed for the crap is a great equalizer. My wife once felt the need while fishing beneath a bridge and, having accomplished the feat, was greeted by loud prolonged applause from two old yokels on the bridge above, who waved a greeting, which she returned with the finger salute.)

The old-style waders had the boots attached, but the new lightweight ones have feet in them like a baby's sleeper, and you put ankle-high boots on over that. What happened to me, first time out, was that my wading boots, being size fourteen, were too big, and kept swallowing up my lightweight waders, pulling them down. Against that was the force of my elastic suspenders, pulling the waders up. I was caught in the middle in particularly sensitive portions of my anatomy. Thus handicapped, it is difficult to walk trails that are full of muck, roots, rocks and debris, and frequented by bears, to boot.

If you fish The Labrador, or anyplace else in Canada, for that matter, you had better know about bears, and have some plan of action when confronted with one—there is an etiquette involved, and bears are anglers, too.

On an early trip to the Old Fort, they shot a four-hundred-pound bear on the beach in front of the camp, the verdict being he was the same bear that wrecked the place each spring, breaking in and throwing provisions all over the place, leaving a clawmark on one wall that remains the camp's main conversation piece, along with a hardcover edition of Lee Wulff's book, *Atlantic Salmon*, which the bear cuffed so hard the claw marks went through the cover, right through to page 172.

Another year there were three bears—papa bear, mama bear, and little baby bear. The outgoing party of Yanks told of seeing papa, all three hundred pounds of him, on their last day in camp, and they saw the tracks of mama and baby all around the campsite. The bears broke into the icehouse and made off with ten of the party's fifty salmon, leaving only forty to be carried back to the U.S.A.

The Yanks wished us luck, and told us not to keep any food in the cabins and not to get between mama and baby, a situation to which female bears have been known to object. And be very careful about going to the outhouse—an encouragement, I confess, to finding quick relief over the verandah rail of the cabin.

We asked proprietor Sam Fequet what to do if we encountered the bears on the trails to the salmon pools, and he said just to stand our ground and c-c-c-lap our h-h-h-hands, the b-b-b-bears would g-g-go aw-w-w-way. And if they tried to break into our sleeping cabin, we were to b-b-beat on the w-w-w-walls with st-st-sticks. He came up with a potty to cut down on the trips to the outhouse.

Every morning there were bear tracks all around the camp—and every morning we set out for the upstream pools with our hair standing on end.

When we returned at day's end with the catch, the guide walked ahead with a fish outstretched, ready to offer it to the first bear, without argument.

We never did have the dreaded face-to-face encounter, and by trip's end, there was the suspicion Sam had shot the bears, even though there was a law against it. Despite a nagging feeling that the bears inhabited this country long before us, we didn't raise the point, accepting the dictum of the wild, that dead bears tell no tales.

I did chide Sam for burying bears without saving at least part of the meat for the sports—bear meat, I have found on the few occasions I have been offered any, makes good eating. I have even had it marinated, though it was not as enjoyable as the fresh kind, and I told Sam that the fat of the bear used to be highly regarded for medicinal purposes, not to mention as slickum for the hair. Anglers of an earlier time, according to their writings, used to lather it on to protect against the flies.

Sam was unmoved, clearly believing that the only good bear was a dead one, and the best place for a dead one was under the ground. When I told him that eastern black bears were softies, compared to western grizzlies, he was unimpressed, though the younger guides seemed interested, since, like all good Eastern Quebeckers and Newfoundlanders, they had dreams of going to the promised land of Calgary, where the jobs were. That there might be bears there, big ones, had not occurred to them, and when I told them about some friends of mine who had been clawed, they seemed impressed, but I think some of them went west anyway.

It was on that bear-y trip that I discovered what may be my most favorite fishing hole of all time, including those dimly-remembered dark places on the brooks of one's youth, where the tug of a trout made you forget all else in life. I knew three such places in New Brunswick, and they must be there yet, though not as vividly as in my dreams.

This place on the Old Fort was at the bottom of one of the portages, and not the sort of place anybody would cast for salmon. But I dappled a dry fly over it while the guide was getting the boat ready, and a beautiful speckled trout took it on the jump. Another dapple, another trout. The action continued for five minutes and then stopped cold, by which time I had six trout. We cooked them on the embers of the lunchtime fire, beside a pool that yielded six salmon that day, and the taste of fresh-broiled trout, wood ashes and all, is with me yet. Every trip since, I have taken our lunchtime trout from that spot, dappling a dry fly—and the bigger and brighter the fly, the better. It helps if you have a dab of butter to put on the trout—the guides usually forget to bring it, because they prefer the condensed milk sandwiches.

Fishing for Atlantic salmon, especially on small rivers, has been likened to big game hunting—you stalk your prey and very often you know exactly where the fish are. You can see them, lying near the bottom of the pool, and often they flash their silver bellies like strobe lights in the depths, and they wave their tails lazily while moving their lips and fanning their gills. Often you can see three or four, or perhaps a dozen of them, at rest in a single pool, and I have read of some of the big pools on the Miramichi where the bottom count ran into the hundreds.

On larger rivers like the Restigouche it is different, especially since the color of the water changes so rapidly, and much of the fishing from the big canoes is "into the brown"—blind casting on a mathematical pattern, designed to pass a fly over a fish wherever it may lie. To my mind this is a form of trolling, the method used in most West Coast salmon fishing, where the location of any given fish is unknown and you hope for the best, the best being if your lure passes through a school of them, in which case the action is fast and furious and likely to be shared by the hundred other boats that flock to the scene, and the catches are the kind you read about. For the most part, though, West Coast fishing can be very leisurely stuff, rods set in holders, drinks in hand, and the quality of the day depending in large measure on the quality of the company, and the food.

The Atlantic salmon, by contrast, provides sport whether on the line or off, and it is a rare angler whose mind remains clear in the middle of a pool of leaping salmon, none of them paying the slightest attention to what is being offered. You feel like a busker on a crowded street when nobody is putting anything in the hat, or the soap box orator whose impassioned words fall on deaf ears.

You are sure you have the right fly on, and that you are presenting it with rare skill and delicacy, and yet the pool explodes with jumping fish and there are no takers.

The first time this happened to me on the Old Fort was during a hatch of spruce budworms, those mothlike creatures that infest the forest and turn the green trees brown. The air was so thick with them it was like a fog, and the first fish they roused were the speckled trout. Unlike most salmon anglers on the Old Fort, we will take trout when they are available, both for the sport and for the eating, but when the trout are having a gorge like this one, they show no appetite whatever for our hair-and-feathers flies. We took not a single trout, and when the salmon started jumping after the trout subsided, it was the same story. It has been well said that jumping fish do not take—I have never known one to do so, but the urge to cast where a salmon has jumped remains irresistible.

Nobody knows why salmon jump in a river, any more than why one takes the fly, since it is agreed that, once they leave the sea for their fresh-water spawning places, they do not eat—the evidence being the empty stomachs of every Atlantic salmon caught and cleaned in Eastern rivers.

One explanation for jumping salmon is that they do it to see where they are going, and to view the scenery. Another is that they want to have a clear look at the idiots who are waving wands at them.

Then there is the sheer-joy theory, related to the idea that a salmon jumps when you hook it because it enjoys the battle as much as the angler does, hence the angler's cry of "Oh, you beauty!" and other exclamations of admiration and comradely affection. My wife says this idea can only be tested if the roles are reversed and the fisherman or woman is on the sharp end, with the salmon holding the rod and playing the human quarry, admiring each wiggle and leap.

When all the salmon in a pool start jumping at the same time, the angler might as well go home, or stay to watch the spectacle and enjoy the scenery.

I was in a pool up to my chest waders when all seven of its finny occupants (of the pool, that is, not my waders) started jumping at the same time, for no reason that I could fathom. Some did it in graceful arcs, some went straight up and bellied back into the water with loud splashes. A couple rose from the surface and danced along it on their tails, the way the porpoises do in the water shows.

Guide D'Arcy Fequet had seen this sort of thing before and he calculated the weight of each fish as they rose, ranging from seven to twelve pounds, the metric system not yet having arrived on the river, and the Yank sports having no comprehension of it, anyway.

I kept trolling my fly through the roiling waters and, while doing so, had the experience of a salmon jumping right under my nose. I made a wild swipe at it with my free hand, seeking to scoop the fish into the top of my waders, with a fine disregard for the predicament that would have ensued. This rise of salmon finished as quickly as it had begun, and the salmon sank to the bottom of the pool. We returned to camp empty-handed, being rewarded on our return by the sight of a black mink, one of nature's wonders. Our admiration subsided somewhat when we were told the mink had invaded the icehouse and made off with a salmon and a large trout.

The home pool beckoned, though I had never seen a salmon taken there. I bet the youngest member of our party ten bucks he couldn't get one and break the day's goose-egg. He took the bet, trotted off (young anglers always trot), and was back in fifteen minutes with a fine grilse, lamenting he hadn't made the bet twenty instead of ten. This young man, Jamie Woods, was the master of the casting technique known as the double haul, which only one of the Fequet boys could match—a bit of artistry that doubles or trebles the length of a cast and gives access to waters denied to older, wiser but weaker anglers. It also results in the many fine flies that repose in the trees along the river, as well as those that snap off from the whiplash, usually flies that I have loaned to the tournament casters.

One more line about jumping salmon—I once heard a Newfoundlander talk about a pool where "they were jumping so high the sky was full of them."

Enough.

We were talking about women on fishing trips, and lucky is the man who has a fishing companion who will sponge his aching body at the end of the first day on the trails, and soothe his bones while tending the cabin fire and mixing drinks, while lighting herself a big cigar after filling a man's pipe. Women must get stiff and sore too, and crave rubs and baths, but they don't seem to feel it as much, or at least they don't complain— perhaps it's just that the ones that do, stay home.

Apart from a muttered "Oh, shit," over a lost fish, my wife is very calm on the waters, and was never more so than in the incident of Mervin's hat.

Mervin was the guide and, like most of his kind, was inclined to festoon his hat with pins, flies and other appendages, making him look like a walking Canadian Tire catalogue. He was proud of that hat, and we had never seen it off his head until the afternoon Claudy hooked into a nice salmon on the upper pool and the fish took a big circular run, passing her line over Mervin's head and whipping off the hat, which hooked itself onto the line.

Mervin, whose job it was to keep track of the fish, switched his priorities to his hat, and gave chase as it slowly slid along the line in the direction of the fighting fish. The harder the fish fought, the faster the hat moved down the line, with Mervin in pursuit until the water reached the top of his hip waders. He stopped, but the hat continued down the line. Madame controlled the fish and was reeling in, with Mervin making wild swipes at the hat with his net.

"Never mind the hat," said Madame, "concentrate on the fish."

Finally, the hat reached the end of the line, just as Claudy brought fish, and hat, within reach of the net. Mervin made a swipe, netted the hat, and in the process released the fish, which stayed at his feet, seemingly dazed by the whole experience.

"Net the fish!" roared Claudy. But Mervin was busy pouring the water out of his hat, inspecting it, and then clamping it back on his head, by which time the salmon had swum leisurely back out into the stream and was gone.

Words failed Madame, in both our maternal languages, unlike another time, when we were fishing in New Brunswick and she gave a political speech in the middle of the Square Forks salmon pool, at the junction of the North and Main Sevogle rivers.

Political talk was hot on that trip, because Madame had been nominated as the Tory candidate in the Gatineau riding of Québec, and an election call was imminent, since John Turner was feeling his oats as the new Liberal Prime Minister of Canada. Claudy's appointed guide for the fishing was an academic named Condé Grondin, a trough Grit (we used the term to counter the more familiar "rabid" Tory) who kept assuring her that she was mad to run in the wrong riding for the wrong party, and that she was going to take a wiping.

She said to him, "Did you come here to talk, or to fish? Please shut up so a Tory can fish, sir!"

She tells it:

We were fishing at the site of an abandoned bridge that was supposed to be a hot spot. We had crossed there in a Jeep on the way into the camp and we got stranded on the rocks in the middle. The water came in, and right into my purse. Condé was the driver, and I held it against him that everything got flooded, including my checkbook, and the pages all got stuck together, wiping out all the entries. Considering my financial habits, this created great havoc, because I now had no idea of what was coming in and what was going out, a bad thing for an election candidate.

I was already ill-disposed toward him, and that night, before we started fishing the Sevogle, I discovered that he was so deep a trough Grit that he had been Executive Assistant to the Liberal leader in the New Brunswick legislature.

Before we started fishing he predicted disaster for the Mulroney Tories, because he felt Richard Hatfield couldn't deliver anything for the federal Tories in New Brunswick. He felt it was a pity that a nice lady like me was going to have her clock cleaned in the election.

The next morning I found, to my shock, that I was to be sent off with Grondin to fish at the Old Bridge, while my husband had choicer waters with another guide. The blackflies were horrible, it being the beginning of July, so I had doused myself totally with flydope. We walked over to the site, and had to wade in on the slippery rocks that had caused the Jeep to get bogged down on our way in. It was not a happy scene.

The first thing that happened was, it became apparent the slippery rocks were treacherous, and Grondin was goading me, picking up the argument from the night before, as we tried to find a good position on the river to make some casts. I was so angry I was stomping, and then I slipped and fell into the fast water, which, of course, washed all the flydope off me. But I riz, brushing off his offers of help, and he said, "Just stand here, and stick your feet between those rocks there."

I did that, and started casting, with the water dripping off the end of my nose.

He started telling me what a good angler I seemed to be, and telling me where I should aim the fly. In my anger I tried to hit the exact spot to spite him, and he said, "Hey, you're pretty good."

He added he didn't understand how anybody who seemed so bright could be a Tory.

That's when I yelled at him, "Fish!"

All of a sudden, we heard a voice coming from the bank. I looked around, and there was a big American standing there, and he said, "I see one! I see one!"

He started giving me orders about where to cast, and Grondin was giving me a hard time about politics. I finally said "Shut up!" to both of them. The American said I was casting too far. I said, "I know what I'm doing," and I cast short, and that's when the salmon took.

The American said, "My God, she's got one!"

He was a live one, and he headed immediately down the river. You could hear the reel going *whir-r-r-r-r-r-r*. I let him have the headway, and Grondin was shouting.

"That's right, that's right, that's right, you got 'im."

Then I felt the salmon stop, and I started reeling him in, and Condé said, "Let's cross the river to the other shore, because there's a branch there he could get hung up on."

He said to reel him in slowly, and I was holding the rod very high in my left hand, my strong one. Grondin was holding my elbow and he was saying, "Cross! Cross!"

All of a sudden, the fish took off again downstream, and we chased after him, up to our necks in white water. The fish was going down, down, and so were we, and we were laughing like loons.

Grondin kept commenting on my gear—the name of the reel (Hardy), and the rod (Eddie Bauer), and he said he thought I had a chance.

All of a sudden the fish swerved to the other side, so I said, "Here's to nothing!" and plunged back into the river. Grondon had no choice but to come too, holding my elbow to keep the rod high.

We crossed the river, and finally we reached a lower pool that is known as the bathtub. We were up to our waists in water and trying not to slip into the bathtub, with me keeping my line taut, and all of a sudden everything went quiet. The fish wasn't moving, the line wasn't moving, we weren't saying anything, and then Grondin whispered, "Reel in slowly."

I did, with my right hand, and he came closer and closer. Condé reached over with the net and plucked him, lifted him, and reached into his pocket for the measuring tape, measured him, and said, "Shit, he's just a little bit over the limit." That meant he would have to go back. He measured again, looked at me and said, "The way you took that fish, you just might win that election." I said to let him go, and he looked at me, and shook the fish off to freedom, and then he turned and hugged me, and said, "That's the most fun I've had in a long, long time."

Grits, after all, don't get that much, says Madame, with that shrug of hers.

It was next day that Madame was fishing the bridge pool, when Grondin appeared on the swinging bridge overhead to shout down that Turner had called the election, adding that this meant Madame's political career was doomed.

"Screw you," she replied, or the French equivalent, and at this point a salmon took her fly and she was locked in combat, meanwhile spouting phrases that would be the backbone of her main campaign speech. She landed the salmon, and she landed the riding, too, even though her face was swollen with blackfly bites from the Sevogle, and she became the first Tory ever to sit for that constituency across the river from Ottawa. Politics and fishing turned out to be a good mix, and eventually even Grondin took a political turn, when his Liberals won every seat in the province and had the fishing all to themselves.

THE BLAMELESS SPORT?

In the matter of fishing being the blameless sport, as St. Peter is reputed to have said, it all depends on what you call blame.

Nobody knows what fish feel, since, while anglers can think like fish, they cannot feel like them.

There is no doubt that, when commercial fishing boats make those big hauls you see in documentaries, the fish that are flashing in the nets are breathing their last, and dying before our eyes. To become part of our food chain, they have to be dead, unlike the way it happens in their watery habitat, where they are eaten alive.

In Nova Scotia's St. Margaret's Bay, a place so beautiful that poets have likened it to heaven, I have accompanied commercial fishermen on hunts for the giant tuna, using as weapons both the harpoon and the axe.

The harpoon proved ineffective, because the tuna moved too fast, and were too smart for us. At one point, our exasperated man in the harpoon pulpit tried to sink his shaft into a loon that was cruising under water, fishing. Happily, the loon had no trouble avoiding the harpoon, being as nimble under water as it is clumsy on shore.

Unhappily for the tuna, though, there are other ways of catching him (fish are always him, at least in story). For the commercial fishermen, there are quicker ways of killing the fish they call the horse mackerel. What is involved is finding the school, the easiest part, because tuna bask and play like dolphin on the surface. Then a bunch of boats string nets all the way around the school and start drawing them in, narrowing the circle until the tuna are concentrated in a narrow space, starting to panic. At this point, the dories enter the confined water, each with an axeman in the prow. The slaughter commences, and it is a fearsome scene, made more so by the flow of blood that turns the foaming water crimson. When the slaughter is over, the tuna are towed ashore to the fish plant, where the axes complete the butchering, and by nightfall the carcasses, some weighing as much as four hundred kilos, are on their way to market. It used to be New York, but later the big money was Japanese.

I do not suppose a fish that weighs four hundred kilos has any more feeling than one that fits the frying pan. It is best not to dwell on the matter, and suppose they act entirely on reflex and have no way of knowing or caring about the kinds of things that bother us.

But any angler who has foul-hooked a fish will know how different it is from catching one fair in the mouth, having tricked the fish into biting on what is on the barbed hook. There are anglers, I know, who file the barbs off the hook to give the fish a better chance, and there are those who cut off two of the three points on a gang hook, and file the barb off the single point remaining, but these knights of the angle are few and need not detain us here.

The foul-hooking of a fish, any fish, involves imbedding the hook in its back, or its belly, or its tail, or anywhere but in its face. Almost always it happens involuntarily, though in the case of poachers, the lordly Atlantic salmon can be snagged in this way, as is described elsewhere in this narrative.

Even a smallish trout that is foul-hooked will put up a tremendous fight before being landed, giving the angler a wild surmise about the size of fish on the line, followed by disappointment when the fight is finished. But it has been a fight, because the fish has had a chance to use its full strength against the pressure of the line, beyond anything it can manage when hooked in the mouth.

An Atlantic salmon that is foul-hooked (often they do it themselves when they rise to a fly and miss it) is deemed a disaster in the angling fraternity, because of the fuss it makes in a pool and the inordinate length of time it takes to land. The pressure a foul-hooked fish can exert is enormous, and if the sport is really the thing, you might think this is just what the angler came for, but no. Fellow anglers will complain that the pool has been riled up for the day, and that the entire episode has been bad luck.

The views of the fish, fair-hooked or fouled, are unknown, but I have a sneaky feeling it is more comfortable to have a hook in your back than in your mouth, though I confess that, having been hooked in both places, neither feels good.

One more thing while we are on the subject of cruelty, and at the risk of having Greenpeace do unto angling what they did to sealing. This is the matter of bait, so it does not concern the fly fishermen and women, who, in any case, regard themselves as above any discussion of what they call meat fishing.

It is not sexist, I hope, to say that few women enjoy the business of putting a worm on a hook. As with fish, the feelings of worms are unrecorded, but they squirm as hard as hooked fish fight, and it may be assumed they do not enjoy the process, even though we know the more they wiggle about, the more they tempt the fish, which is the very thing we are after.

Similarly, the fixing of a minnow on a hook is not the sort of thing you would do at a formal dinner, and still less is the baiting of a hook with a live frog. Sometimes, these creatures, when used for bait, can be fitted into a harness to which the hooks are attached, and this seems more humane, or it did until I witnessed the business of the harnessed mouse.

We were going for bass near Bedford Mills in Eastern Ontario, and the river, as with most waters in those parts, was clogged with weeds, through which channels had been cut so boats could pass. The trick was to fish in those channels, which required casting as skilled as the drives of pro golfers on TV.

My friend, a native of the region, had brought along a shoe box in which there were several mice, which he had caught in his Havaheart humane trap, the kind that inflicts no harm and enables the quarry to be released. It is never clear where the release is supposed to be made, but having employed these devices in my time, I confess to having released mice in parking lots, the back yards of neighbours I did not like and, on one unforgettable occasion, in some bushes beside a parked tourist bus in Gatineau Park, unaware that a female tourist of a certain age was relieving herself behind that self-same bush. When my liberated mouse ran between her legs, she let out a howl I can hear to this day, and I fled before she could find her voice to accuse me. What would have been the charge, I wonder?

Anyway, my friend with the mousebox threw out the anchor, rummaged in his gear for the device he called his harness, and reached in for a mouse, which he proceeded to fasten into the harness with snaps.

I thought he was going to cast the mouse, live, through the air, but it was not that simple. He had brought along a bundle of small cedar shingles, the kind that are used as shims in the carpentry business, and he placed the harnessed mouse on one of these, setting it gently in the water. The current carried it slowly away from the boat, and my friend paid out the line so delicately that the mouse was able to keep its place on the shingle until it was a good twenty or thirty meters away.

Suddenly, my friend gave a pluck on his line and there was a splash in the distance, when the mouse hit the water and began to struggle, setting up a fuss. *BAM!* A bass hit, and the game was afoot. In came bass, mouse and all. That mouse made two more shingle voyages before it gave up the ghost. (Do mice have feelings? Cats must know, but then we are not even sure about cats.) We then resorted to conventional casting, and caught no more bass, though we brought in tonnes of weeds.

Is there cruelty in any of this?

Could St. Peter have been wrong?

POWER FISHING

I f there's a side of the Canadian establishment that hasn't had the attention it deserves, it's the fishing side.

Much has been made of the way the elite meet in clubs, and boardrooms, and in secret corporate and family conclaves, and a lot has been said about golf and squash and horses, and their place in the economic life of the country. But what happens while bigwigs are fishing may exceed all of these in importance.

In global terms, we have been called hewers of wood and drawers of water, omitting to mention that our waters are also providers of fish that bring great tycoons from around the world to wet their lines. Few American moguls of consequence have failed to fish Canadian lakes or streams for our trout or salmon, and the existence of most of our commercial outfitters and the most famous of our fishing clubs has depended for a century and more on the support of tycoons from the United States who, in many cases, admit Canadians into their circle to provide political balance.

In many ways, it's like Alberta oil—the resource would not have been developed without American know-how and money, and many wealthy Americans know as much about angling as they do about business, which is a great deal. Not infrequently, their women are as skilled on the waters as their men, something that is true of the British angling classes as well, though it is only beginning to come into fashion among the Canadian fishing fraternity/sorority.

There exists an international power network of anglers, and to examine Canada's leading part in it, we turn our attention to leading Canadians who have made angling an essential part of their adult lives.

Simon Reisman has been public servant, businessman, negotiator *par excellence* and *extraordinaire*. He's the fighting cock with the crest of wavy white hair, and a nose for a deal only slightly less sensitive than his nose for a fish. He reads salmon pools with the same eye he uses on financial statements, and he is a familiar figure on the country's choicest waters—a living example of how one salmon leads to another, and how to win friends and influence people while fishing. I have had my best salmon fishing in his company, and we have fished the Arctic waters for trout and grayling, and spent many an evening swapping yarns, without him ever giving me a government or corporate secret. The bond is fishing, with touches of vodka and single malt whisky.

When I sounded out Simon about this book, seeking some of his fish stories, he leapt at it with a "Hey! Maybe we can get some good fishing out of these birds!"

He took it like a rolling salmon takes a fly, and started reeling out the line. It was winter, so maybe they would pay for some fishing off Florida, eh? That was pure Simon—first things first, the main chance, if not for profit, then for pure joy. What better sport than fishing with all expenses paid, and spinning yarns in the evening?

It would be money for jam for me, and fun for him, and he rubbed his hands until I cooled him out with my reply.

I said I doubted it, since publishers were more inclined to take fishing trips than to give them. What they wanted were the fish stories already in our memory banks, and I had been at it most of my life, while Simon had done more power fishing than any other man alive, if you define power fishing as fishing with the powerful.

There is a theory that Simon became powerful through fishing, but this is an exaggeration. Fishing was just one of many weapons he used in moving from the slums of east-end Montreal to high places in government, business and diplomacy. The most spectacular of those weapons were a sharp wit and a sharp tongue and knowing, like the gambler he is, when to hold 'em, and when to fold 'em.

Through many years of friendship, Reisman and I have skirted the barrier that is supposed to exist between the people who make the news and the people who report it. He has endured without open complaint some of the things I have written about him, including a blast about taking retirement on full pension at age fifty-five, which he was fully entitled to do as Deputy Minister of Finance, but my bleat was that the country was entitled to the benefit of his wisdom to age sixty-five, instead of which he hung out his shingle in the marketplace.

He prospered, and there came the day when he was appointed ambassador to negotiate Canada's free trade agreement with the United States, and I wrote that, if the Yanks wanted to appeal to Reisman's weak spot, they would invite him fishing. I had fished enough with him to know that he had one rule about fishing—go if invited, and fish hard, and yield nothing to the host, much less to the critics, with their "conflict of interest" charges at the ready. Fishing as sin is not in Bible, Torah or Koran, though poaching may be, and my advice to the Americans was to get our man Reisman away on the waters, but not to expect him to concede anything of substance on the business at hand. They never tried, and I assumed it was because all the good fishing is in Canada, anyway, and Reisman had ready access to most of it.

The real reason, Simon tells me now in some anguish, was that Uncle Sam appointed, as chief U.S. trade negotiator, an unknown named Peter Murphy, who, besides being half Reisman's age, had no direct access to the top rungs of government and, more seriously, did not smoke, drink, play poker or fish. The only recreation Murphy enjoyed, so far as Reisman could determine, was softball—so Reisman dutifully appeared on television, trying to hold his own at the plate and running out a grounder.

In terms of fishing, though, the free trade negotiations were not a total loss, thanks to the tendency in Canada for all problems to boil down to decisions over federal and provincial jurisdictions. The United States might not have Atlantic salmon-fishing to offer, but the negotiations did involve something called the Federal-Provincial Continuing Committee on Trade Negotiations, and out of that, in the heat of the free trade battle, Reisman got invitations from the governments of Québec and New Brunswick to fish their waters. Thus it was that important aspects of free trade policy were hammered out on the St. John and the York in Québec's Gaspé, and at Larry's Gulch on New Brunswick's Restigouche.

On arrival at the Québec government camp on the St. John—Saint-Jean now—Reisman encountered the incoming party of anglers led by Gil Remillard, the Québec minister then in charge of Québec's part in the Meech Lake Accord. It was on those storied waters that policies were shaped both on the constitution and the free trade agreement with the United States. They should put up a cairn, or something.

"We learned later that, with a change in the weather and the water level, the Remillard party had good fishing," Reisman recalls, "and we didn't do so well. But free trade fared better in the end than Meech Lake." It was on the York, though, that Simon saw the biggest salmon of his life, estimated by the guides to weigh seventy pounds. "He was one of a bunch lying at the foot of some low cliffs, and they looked like logs. I dappled a fly over them but there was no way of playing them if they took, which none of them did. But the sight was worth the trip."

Simon's mention of the deep canyons of the York triggered my memory, and I dug out an old account, dated 1876, and

Simon

read it to him on a subsequent evening. It described that same spot, with 150 salmon at rest—only on this occasion the angler went to an accessible pool above, and in three hours took five salmon, totalling 112 pounds. Two years before, in 1874, an angler killed eighteen heavy fish at that same spot and floated them back to camp on a raft. That early account of fishing on the York and St. John is heavy with references to the adventures of the Earl and Countess of Dufferin on the York and St. John, the Countess being an accomplished angler, it being noted that, "when ladies fish, a smudge is kept burning upon a flat stone in the canoe," to keep the flies off.

The Dufferins were part of a long line of Governors General and their spouses who have enjoyed the salmon fishing in Québec and New Brunswick—none savored it more than the British appointees who were accustomed to the angling in Scotland and Ireland as a regular thing, and had whole Canadian rivers at their command. Canadian-born viceroys may not have kept up the tradition, but Canadian politicians and mandarins, federal and provincial, have taken it over, both for business and pleasure.

Pleasure is the operative word, and when you ask Simon why he fishes so much, he comes back with, "Because it's fun!"

Yet he fishes as intensely as he negotiates, or as he plays poker, or as he does just about everything in life, from his honors in university and his overseas Second World War service with the Royal Canadian Artillery in Italy and Europe, to a meteoric public-service career that saw him in the top jobs in three senior departments of government (Industry, Treasury Board and Finance), before taking an early quit.

It was as much fascination as friendship that made me a fan of Simon the fisherman, and going to the fishing, and coming home from it we would exchange yarns, and he would give his unvarnished views of the people and events around him, often with himself as the storm center.

As for his regard for me, it defies explanation, unless it has something to do with the bond that used to exist between ignorant Irish and smart Jews—the sort of thing that was celebrated in the old American stage chestnut, *Abie's Irish Rose*.

Certainly it was not any special regard Simon had for my profession, because most of my colleagues were openly out to get the man they called "that little son of a bitch." One of the most vivid exchanges during the Canada-U.S. free trade negotiations was when Reisman, on camera in Washington, called Bob Hepburn, of *The Toronto Star*, a hack working for a rag.

Reisman and Hepburn didn't fish together, nor, so far as I know, did Simon fish with news people other than myself. He did fish with U.S. negotiator John Connolly, but Reisman regarded Connolly as an equal.

In all the exchanges I have had with Simon, he has not given me any secrets or scoops worth noting, and I do not believe I have violated the unwritten codes of my trade. Most of our talk has been, not about great affairs, but about great fishing, and few men know more about that than Simon, who has fly fished just about every notable stretch of speckled trout and Atlantic salmon water in a country that has the world's best angling for both species. Québec has the trout franchise, and shares the salmon honors with New Brunswick, Nova Scotia and Newfoundland and Labrador, and Reisman has been thrashing all those waters for the best part of forty-five years, usually as the guest of sponsors who must have been hoping to gain a favor, with no evidence that they ever did. Usually, Reisman responds by giving them a shellacking at the poker table, and the higher the stakes, the better he likes it.

Hearing Reisman on poker tells you a lot about the way he conducts a negotiation, whether it be with humans, or fish. Here's what he says.

I am a very conservative poker player. I don't play every hand, by any means, and I don't bluff very often. Not very often, more seldom than most. And that's why, when I do bluff, usually it works. But if I have a hand that I think has got a good chance of winning, I'll play that hand for everything it's worth. You know, for everything it's worth. I believe in exploiting your opportunities and avoiding excessive risk.

That's how I play poker, and I can tell you that I win three times out of five anyway. Perhaps a little better than that. And on balance, I'll be a winner in that kind of game. But it's not through a lot of bluffing, not through that. I just do very little of that. But I plan very aggressively and I make my good cards pay.

The size of the stakes doesn't bother me at all. I much prefer to play a table-stakes game than a limited game of poker. Because the only way you can really protect a good hand is to bet your hand high. Otherwise, you know, if people can afford to come in, if every grocery clerk can come in there at small risk and challenge your hand, you are going to lose now and then. So, when I have a good hand, I like to be able to bet it very hard, and open stakes is what I like. Table stakes. There they are. The limit is what you have on the table. In a table-stakes game, people put their poke on the table and they can be called for that, or they can bet that at any time in a game, but they cannot replenish in the middle of a hand.

Once you have exhausted your poke, then there are side stakes, and you're in for what you bet for and the others go on with the larger game. That is really the only way to play poker, in my view.

End of lesson.

I had fished enough with Simon to know that the way he fishes is not all that different from the way he plays poker, which led me to wonder if his negotiating techniques follow the same pattern, leading governments, clients and even feuding families to beat a path to his door.

Over another drink, he put it this way.

You'll have to ask other people about how I negotiate. I am very much an above-board negotiator. I don't make a great mystery of what my objectives are. I try, early in a negotiation, to try to get some kind of an understanding and agreement as to what it is we are trying to reach, and I don't make it a mystery.

Sometimes people on the other side kind of wonder, and as often as not they don't believe me, and sort of feel that, classically, negotiations are as much about concealing as revealing. But I can tell you that I am very much an open and above-board negotiator, but very determined.

I suppose if I were to talk about one rule above all other rules that I try to apply in a negotiation, it is this: I never go into a negotiation with the sense that I have got to have an agreement. Never.

I go into a negotiation wanting to succeed, and having a pretty good sense as to what a minimum good agreement is, and I won't settle for anything else.

I'll tell you what a negotiation is really about. You set your objectives, and you know what you must have as a minimum. And then you know what you would like to have beyond that.

And then you make a judgment about the other fellow, about what his objectives are, what he will accept as a minimum. Now, if his minimum and your minimum can be encompassed by his terms of reference and yours, then the negotiation is about what you can add of yours, and he no doubt looks at what he can add of his, and it is that little bit of stuff that the negotiation is really about, the basis stuff having really been established by the initial minimum requirements.

It is exceedingly important to know the other fellow, so you can make judgments about that. I never go into a negotiation feeling that I must have an agreement, because if you do, you almost always get a bad agreement.

I have watched negotiators do that, over and over again, winding up with much less than was available, or if not, settling for an agreement that is really not a good agreement, having regard to the essential interests of a party to the negotiation.

So that's my first and most fundamental rule—you musn't feel you have got to have an agreement. You've got to be prepared to walk away.

Oh, yeah. I'm prepared not to complete an agreement, and go in quite prepared not to accept an agreement that does not accept your minimum requirements.

On the occasion of the free trade negotiations with the United States, I wasn't certain what the outcome was going to be, when I walked out. In my heart, I believed, and I told the prime minister, that I thought this was the only way we could shake them up.

We had to do that before they realized what the game was really about, because, for one reason or another, they had gone into the negotiation believing that we had to have an agreement.

The Americans believed that, and they played it accordingly. So on that day we walked away and, if the Americans hadn't come back, that would have been the end. It was for them to come back. We walked away, and I can tell you they were shaken to their bootstraps, and when I say they, I mean the top authorities, Jim Baker, who was the chairman of the economic policy committee of the cabinet, and he was playing it very cool and wouldn't be engaged.

We tried many times—the prime minister tried at many summits, and George Bush was involved on one occasion—and it didn't do a damn bit of good.

This time, we got their attention.

I jumped in to turn the talk back to fishing, and Simon laughed and likened it to a time he was on the Eagle River with his one-time commanding officer, Lieutenant-General W.A.B. Anderson, and Anderson was into a salmon that went to the bottom of the pool and wouldn't move.

"Watch this," said Anderson, pulling a knife out of his pocket and tapping it sharply on the butt of his rod. The taps sent a signal to the salmon below, and there was a tremendous surge in the water beside the boat, as the fish leaped straight in the air and landed in the bottom of the boat at Anderson's feet.

"Sometimes the shock treatment works," said Simon, reaching for a cigar, and then remembering that he had given them up.

I asked Simon to relate his poker and negotiating philosophies to fishing, especially on those bad days when there are no fish.

"I've had lots of those," said Simon. The first rule was to keep fishing. He went on.

I've been skunked on quite a few occasions. I don't mean a day's skunking, that's occurred very often. I'm talking about a whole trip. I've been skunked totally and entirely, especially in Nova Scotia. Nova Scotia is a very tough province for salmon fishing. The first time was on the Salmon River on the Eastern Shore, near the St. Mary.

I was skunked on the Salmon River, and skunked on the St. Mary, and I fished four days on the one and maybe three days on the other. Skunked! Then, on one occasion, I fished the Margaree for six days with Doug Fullerton and guys from the Cape Breton Development Corporation, and we had a very good guide, who knew the river very well. We worked hard at it and we got up early, trying to get there before other fishermen, though that was very difficult on that river, and I was skunked. I didn't see a fish.

Nobody did. The entire party.

Yet I enjoyed the trip, I remember it, I remember the pools. There were some pools there, you were certain there would be a strike on every cast. Nothing. It is a magnificent river. We fished not far from the museum, surrounded by grand pools.

It wasn't just Nova Scotia with bad fishing. One year, I was skunked completely and entirely on the Sainte-Marguerite, my favorite of all rivers in Québec, or anywhere else. Fishing went down dismally there, but there has been a revival in the last half-dozen years. This particular year, though, the entire party fished four days, six rods, and caught only one grilse.

This was in 1978, twenty-four years after I first fished on that river. Since then, though, I have never fished on the Sainte-Marguerite that I didn't get my fish per day, which is the limit. Unfortunately, it's a fish a day whether it's a salmon or a grilse, and you know what that leads to—you try very hard not to land a grilse, and you would be amazed how hard it is to lose a fish when you want to.

How can a man who comes on so strong, enjoy a lifetime of fishing, a sport that involves more contemplation than live action? Simon Reisman is a talkative man, and yet he talks very little while fishing, at least with me.

He told me once about taking Marc Lalonde fishing, when Lalonde was Principal Secretary to Prime Minister Pierre

Trudeau, and regarded by many as Trudeau's alter ego. Reisman, as deputy minister of finance, was eager for more insight into what made Trudeau tick, as who wasn't then (or now, for that matter.)?

Lalonde had never fished salmon, but agreed to go with Reisman on a trip to the Whale and Wheeler rivers, in the Ungava, which involved camping under canvas. The first day, Simon and Marc shared a pool, and Simon was showing his guest the rudiments of casting and the proper presentation of the fly.

While giving the instructions, Simon said, "Look, you don't have to answer this if you don't want to, but what is Trudeau really like at home?"

Lalonde was puzzled. "I'm sure I don't know," he said. "I've never been in his home."

Reisman tried again. "What's he like with your children?"

"He's never met my children."

"Truthfully?"

"God's truth."

End of conversation, and the rest of the trip was devoted to fishing, which Lalonde learned to do very well. So well, in fact, that in another year, on another trip and another river, Lalonde caught his limit of two salmon while Reisman was fishing on empty, and when Simon hooked a fish and lost it, Lalonde counselled that Simon was fishing too hard, and putting too much pressure on his fish. It was a case of pupil turned master.

"But Simon," I put in, "you do fish hard, just like you do everything."

He laughed, and we poured ourselves another.

I suppose that I play hard, I work hard, and I come on pretty strong in virtually all my relationships, stronger than I think I do. But people tell me I do. It is a matter of personality. If I have a task to perform, I go at it pretty hard. Maybe because I'm a lazy man. I want to get it over with. In many instances, you have a job to do, tackle it, and get it done, and get on to other things. But then I get on to the other things, and I'll go at them in just as enthusiastic a way.

You ask me why do I do that? The fact is I do that, and sometimes I'll lose a fish because of it. I've lost fish because I've had them on too long. This is particularly true with the younger fish. Once they have a good firm mouth, and once you get that fly firmly into their jaw, unless you've tied the fly badly or some accident occurs, you're going to get that fish. But with the younger fish, or certainly with fish under ten pounds, or grilse, if you have that hook in long, or if it's a double-barbed hook, you're going to work a hole in him, and lose him.

That's one reason why I go at a fish so hard. The other is ... well, you know, there's a fish, and there you are into him, and even if it's catch–and–release, the purpose is, you hook him, to bring him to shore. And, as you know, in New Brunswick today it's all catch–and–release, and the shorter the play the better chance the fish has.

I will land a fish about a third faster than most fishermen, and I think my percentage is better than the ones who play the fish longer and give them less pressure, and I'm sure I have as much fun as they do, and maybe more.

SIMON'S SCORE

I asked Simon how many salmon fishing trips he had been on, up to now.

The number he came up with was seventy.

And how many salmon had he caught?

Well, most trips were for a week, and he figured he had spent at least three hundred days fishing for salmon. He might have been skunked fifty of those days, no more.

"I would be surprised," said he, "if I haven't killed 500 salmon and released another 250. And for every salmon hooked and released, for every three brought to the net, I've lost one through accident or stupidity. I guess I've been into a thousand fish, not counting the ones just pricked and never seen."

To me, these figures were as impressive as those in any federal budget, and Reisman had been the architect of many of those, including some right after the war that resulted in surpluses in the federal treasury. "No trick there," said Reisman, "they just kept the wartime taxes on after the war was over—duck soup." I asked him for some more fishing statistics.

"I have two thousand salmon flies, and a lot more for trout. I keep the salmon flies in boxes, according to the rivers I fish, since each river has its own menu, flywise. When I know what river I'm going to, I'll take that box, along with some trout flies, and then always my own favorite flies, no matter where I'm going. I bought most of my flies on the rivers, except the Sainte-Marguerite, where as a guest you never pay for anything."

Simon has three rods that he uses for salmon, and four trout rods, and ten more salmon rods that were accumulated in his forty years of serious fishing. His three active rods are all by Orvis—a boron of eight and a half feet, a graphite of ten feet, and a bamboo that he uses on small salmon, especially on the Jupiter on Anticosti Island, where most fish are under twelve pounds.

He got that faraway look in his eye. "I always use that bamboo rod for dry fly fishing.

"I was looking at the old rods just this morning—two of them are fibreglass, and they feel heavy now, but they've caught a lot of fish for me. They sit in one room in the basement, and that's where I keep the waders, vests, trousers and jackets, along with the current rods, in a package I rarely undo. I just take the rods out when I get to the river, and the package stays bound up—I don't use fancy packages, but the rods are the best. Fancy packages mean the rods don't often get there, if you know what I mean."

Of all the fish he has caught, Simon had only one mounted, and it's in that basement room, his son having declined it as a gift, deeming it "dumb." It is a trout of six and a half pounds that he caught on the Manitou River on the St. Lawrence north shore, a river that has a steep waterfall at its mouth, which keeps salmon from going up and trout from going down. Simon describes the trout of the Manitou as Québec Reds, though we have never agreed on what a Québec Red is, and my own theory is it is the kind we call the Marstoni, which occurs in a certain lake north of Ottawa. Trouble is, the Marstoni has a silver skin and white flesh, and the only thing red about it is the base of its fins. On the Manitou, where he was the guest of an American paper company, Simon fished with a spinning rod and large lures, because the trophy fish wouldn't go for flies. The stuffed trout is covered with dust, and Simon admits that, though he belongs to two trout clubs, he doesn't enjoy trout fishing all that much, which is a penalty most anglers pay when they get the Atlantic salmon bug.

"Except," Simon hastened to add, "that I've had some wonderful trout fishing when I fish salmon. That happens on the Sand Hill in Labrador, and the Jupiter on Anticosti. I fish for the trout when I've had my day's bag of salmon, or when the trout are in they take all the time, and I like having them for breakfast—I'll feed the whole camp. The guides insist you use flies that won't attract the salmon, like the Parmachene Belle, but of course, when the salmon really want to take, they'll grab those too.

"And the Muddler Minnow works on everything. I've had very good luck with muddlers, on trout and salmon. My favorite is the gold, on a Number 8 hook, especially when nothing else works. It's rarely my first choice—the guide tells me what's best for that—but if things are slow, the Muddler's not long in coming out of the box."

POLITICS

One of the hardest things to believe in our times together wasn't a fish story at all—it was Simon saying he liked being alone.

I couldn't imagine Simon Reisman without somebody to talk to, somebody to ask those questions that start, "You don't have to answer this if you don't want to..."

"My best times have been alone," he said. "Especially trout fishing, out on a lake, alone with just the quietness of the lake. And I like to be alone when I'm salmon fishing, too, but that hardly ever happens, because you always have to have a guide, and sometimes, on a strong river, it's not such a great idea to be by yourself."

"You," I said, "are the most gregarious man I've ever known."

"Not really," he laughed. "I like parties and I like a lot of people, but I like being alone."

"You're talking like Trudeau," I said, "and you're not like him at all. Trudeau hates fishing."

What made me say that was a recollection from some press conference, or someplace, of Trudeau expressing distaste for trying to hook a fish in the mouth.

"Don't write that," said Reisman. "Trudeau fished salmon on the Jupiter; I've seen the pictures in the book there. He took his son fishing with him, and he took fish."

"Did he ever go back?"

"Well, Pierre doesn't like to repeat things. He went fishing, and he got fish, and maybe that was enough."

Reisman knew John Turner better, having served as his deputy minister when Turner was Minister of Finance, and having acted as adviser to Turner when he succeeded Trudeau as Liberal leader and prime minister. Simon came on strong.

John Turner is a good fisherman—very, very good on a river. Very competitive. Turner and Trudeau didn't like each other, and Turner always thought he was a better man than Trudeau—he resented Trudeau staying around as long as he did.

And Trudeau was very envious of Turner—his good looks, his obvious charm, the ease with which he could move in every circle. I think Trudeau is a remarkable guy, but he wasn't a man who had great self-confidence.

Arrogant? You should know that people behave like that, not because they have infinite self-confidence, it's because they lack it. With Trudeau, a lot of it is perverse. This guy could lack confidence and be shy of meeting people, and at the same time, have contempt and disdain for most of them.

Think back to Turner, before his successive defeats. Turner, in the end, revealed himself as human, after all—with human frailties—and that disappointed many admirers. But in his earlier days, his best years as minister of finance, that was the John Turner that Pierre Trudeau envied. Able to command respect in the cabinet, speak well, never make mistakes, eyes in the back of his head, and a hell of a ladies' man.

He was ambitious, and had great expectations for a full political career. I had a lot of regard for him, he was tremendous in terms of capacity to work, discipline and orderliness. I always gave him credit for being able to select people, but it turned out that wasn't really his strong suit, after all. He just happened to get lucky with people he inherited while a Minister of the Crown.

As a cabinet minister, he had three good deputies, including me in finance—top-notch people, who served him well. If you wrote good music, he certainly knew how to play it.

He knew how to use his staff, and made large demands upon them. He would ask for all kinds of help inside the office. One time, early in his finance ministry, he was going to have lunch at the Bank of Canada, and he said to me, "You know all the people. They'll ask me to say a few words, and it would be nice if I could remember their names and say something that would be relevant to what they are doing in the institution." Now, that's not an easy thing to do for somebody else. It's a lot easier to write a substantive speech than a bit of humor, but I would do this for him. I was good at that. I would work at it at home. And then I heard back from somebody I knew well at the bank, who said, "My, he's a remarkable man. You know, they asked him to say a word or two, and he made the most delightful speech, remembered everyone around the table, had an appropriate *bon mot* for each of them."

But as party leader, he needed people to write the music, and he himself didn't know how to get such people. He wasn't rusty, he was just badly served, and I don't think he was as good a judge of horse-flesh as I imagined.

But he goes fishing, and he brings them in.

Simon was going good, so I decided to pump him about a legend attached to his name—that he had butted a live cigar on the U.S. Secretary of the Treasury's desk, a Revolutionary War antique.

The man was John Connolly, who, as Governor of Texas, was in the assassination car with John F. Kennedy, and was gravely wounded in the shooting. As Secretary of the Treasury, he was always at odds with Canadian policy, regarding Canada as fair game for tariff discrimination, suspicious of the floating Canadian dollar (he called it a dirty float) and above all, convinced the Canada-U.S. auto pact was a Reisman plot. All this was raised at the meeting to deal with U.S. import surcharges.

The negotiations were hot and heavy, with Canada seeking relief from U.S. trade surcharges, and the crucial meeting was in Connolly's office in Washington.

John Turner and Simon Reisman

Reisman had a big cigar going, as he usually did under pressure, and he leaned forward to knock off the ash into Connolly's ashtray. "I missed the ashtray," says Simon, "sprinkling ash over the mahogany desktop. I got out my handkerchief and mopped up the ash, shaking it into the wastebasket, amid a horrified silence. And that became the legend of how I butted my cigar on the Alexander Hamilton desk. I never did—there wasn't a live ash in the bunch, but it may have given us an edge—we got the concession."

Years later, Reisman fished with Connolly on the Jupiter River, as guests of Montréal industrialist Paul Desmarais.

"Paul became very friendly with a number of Texas oilmen," Simon recalls. "People like Bill Fuller and Perry Bass. Fuller was a friend of Connolly's and brought him along on the fishing trip. Strange bunch of Texans on a Québec river—all very earnest, strange people—none of them took a drink, they didn't even swear."

I said that was hardly typical of Texans, to judge by Lyndon B. Johnson.

"Well," said Simon, "I'm talking about the ones Desmarais invited to the Jupiter. Connolly was very friendly and we talked about our negotiating sessions.

"Paul asked Connolly about the relationship between the businessmen and government, and how hard it was to establish communications. Connolly had taken to calling me Cy, and he told Desmarais, "If you want to relate to government, what you do is get a good guy like Cy here, and that'll look after your relations. It's that simple."

"I could have kissed Connolly on both cheeks that night for the endorsement. I've done a lot of work for Paul Desmarais, and he's a very good fellow to consult with. Very demanding, respectful, doesn't get you to do a lot of donkey work for him. When he wants something, he wants it now, and wants it good."

And, Simon might have added, he provides good fishing.

I tried to press my luck, by getting Simon to tell me his opinion of Mordecai Richler, and his book, *Solomon Gursky Was Here*, which is filled with references to salmon fishing.

"Let's leave him out," said Simon, without enthusiasm. Both he and Richler were products of the same rough end of Montreal, and it was interesting that both had taken so strongly to angling when they got prosperous.

"Well," said Simon after a long pause, "I know he has fished the Grand Cascapedia as a guest of Frank Moores, and he took a nice big salmon out, and I know the pool out of which he took it, the Mrs. Guest pool, the only one that was producing that year. So he fell in love with the sport, but it was a late revelation. His references in the book to salmon fishing are very amateurish and a little bit naive, and the story about loading the fish with stones to make them weigh more, he got gossiping with guides. I've heard about that happening, but I wouldn't do it myself."

WHY FISHING?

I f Mordecai Richler came to fishing late, Sol Simon Reisman came to it early, which was odd for a kid from the slums of Montréal, until you know that his Ukrainian Jewish mother loved the countryside and always found somewhere in the Laurentians for the family to spend July and August, the machinist father coming up by train for weekends. Simon was born in June of 1919, when his mother was nineteen, and two weeks later they were summering on a farm at Belisles Mill near Val David.

They went there every summer after that, and Simon's first fishing was in a local brook, for suckers and sunfish, using cherrywood poles and grocers' string, with hooks they bought four for a cent.

"Worms," he recollects as the bait, "until we graduated to grasshoppers when we found they'd GET them. Mother welcomed the fish and made gefilte fish that we loved."

At age nine, Simon's fishing moved to the North River, where he caught more suckers, the occasional bass, and eventually his first trout. "The trout was so pretty I just sat and looked at it," he says, "and from then on, I fished with a bamboo pole that cost ten cents, with a cork for a bobber. Most of the fishing was on dull, rainy days, because on nice days we'd swim or play baseball or go exploring in the woods."

In those woods they would find branches just right for slingshots, and with old shoe tongues and inner tubes they would fashion weapons for frog hunting, running up a big score.

"Eat 'em?"

"Nope. Just killed 'em."

There were contests to see who could carve the fanciest stick of spruce, but mainly Simon remembers a little stream that flowed into the North River, which contained small speckled trout in the dark places under the banks.

"Those ones," he remembers, "we would take home and eat whole, fried in butter."

Simon started working at fifteen and his fishing fell off, and when he did fish it was all with bait. He didn't see a fly fisherman until he was twenty, and that was the first time he saw a steel rod with a fly reel on it. It was a memory he carried with him during his years of wartime service in the artillery, but his interest was not revived until after the war, when he joined the Department of Finance, and somebody sent him a fishing catalogue from France, containing what was to become the postwar sensation of fishing, the spinning reel, which, with the Mepps lure, is France's great contribution to the sport. Simon wrote away for some of the French gear and, when it arrived, his serious fishing began. He was thirty years old, and was on the fast track in Finance. His fishing companions were fellow public servants Frank Stone, Jake Warren and Doug Fullerton.

They scoured the Gatineaus for bass and trout, and wherever a lumber company had timber limits, they would encroach—braving flies so fierce that Simon remembers once, on a stream called Kennedy's Creek, having to take to the water up

to his eyeballs to keep from being eaten alive, and trudging down the stream at peril of drowning, rather than face the bugs.

Fly fishing came later—Reisman and Stone were in Geneva as part of a Canadian delegation at a conference on the General Agreement on Tariffs and Trade, and Stone suggested going after grayling in a fast section of the Rhone. They went, and Reisman made a botch of his first fly fishing attempts, and was ashamed.

But when he got home, word had spread that he had done some fly fishing, so he was invited to the Five Lakes Fishing Club in the Gatineaus, as a guest of U.S. Diplomat Woody Willoughby. On that first visit, he was introduced to the Chief Executive Officer of the Aluminum Company of Canada, Scotty Bruce, and Bruce asked if Simon would like to fish at his club on the Sainte-Marguerite, for salmon.

Reisman's eyes sparkle when he tells the story, because that was the magic moment, the entrée into the wonderful world of salmon fishing. He can still remember the tingle at the prospect, and the fear of making a muck of it, as he had on the Rhone, after the grayling.

And he recalls the part that chance played in his encounter with Bruce, illustrating his point that one of the best ways to get invited to fish is to talk about it.

"Not only that," he says, "you'd be surprised at what kind of information comes from a conversation that starts with fishing. It kind of loosens things up."

The introduction to the Sainte-Marguerite certainly loosened up Simon Reisman, starting with a May phone call from Bruce, inviting him to "come fishing and be my guest."

From Ottawa, it was train to Montréal, Canada Steamships to Québec, with an overnight pause before sailing on to Murray Bay, where there was a reception for the fishing party at the posh residence of David Culver. It was at that reception that Reisman first met Paul Desmarais, on his own way to fame and fortune and copious salmon fishing.

From Tadoussac, at the mouth of the Saguenay, cars took the party to a point on the Sainte-Marguerite where they were met by guides with canoes. There were two guides to a canoe, a total of twelve guides for six fishermen.

Simon says you talk about your first salmon river the way you talk about your first love, and when I reminded him that talking about a first love isn't such a great idea in the presence of later ones, he laughed. "Well, at least, you dream about it."

He dreams about the Sainte-Marguerite, and when he talks about it his eyes sparkle, and you believe him when he says he can remember every pool and riffle. He had never seen such a camp. Like so many such places in Canada, it had been built by rich Americans from Boston in the 1860s, when fishing trips could extend as long as five or six weeks. Eventually, it was acquired by ALCAN, whose officers used it for themselves and their guests—"Scotty was our host, and the guests were people who deserved to be invited salmon fishing."

The year was 1954. The rods that were provided were the two-handed variety, fourteen feet long. The lines were of silk, and the leaders were catgut. Each fishermen got a box of flies, and Simon remembers what they were—the Black Dose, the Jock Scott, the Rusty Miller, the Green Highlander, the Nighthawk and the Silver Doctor. The invitation was for a week's fishing, and the limit at the time was four salmon per rod per day, with grilse not included in the count.

Reisman's army experience prepared him for the way the camp was run, because military officers' messes provided the pattern. These posh fishing clubs are an extension of the downtown clubs that exist in every Canadian and American city, and which, in turn, were inspired by the gentlemen's clubs in England, the original ideas for which came from the British army and navy. The basic idea was to make oneself as comfortable as possible whatever the circumstances, and to observe a code of conduct that would be unspoken, but known to all—the best guest test being "any fella you'd have in your own home."

The rustic clubhouses on Canadian rivers and lakes housed the privileged in the rough, keeping in mind the the words of a writer a century ago. "Standing for six hours or more daily while throwing a fly or killing a fish is hard work for one of sedentary habits, and gives enough exercise and oxygen to entitle to good living and quarters."

The best of these places, provided they haven't burned to the ground, are heritage buildings, miniatures of the vast log chateau at Montebello, Québec. The wooden walls have a warm glow and there is a settled quality about everything, including the favorite chairs of members, the paintings and trophies on the walls, the tinkle of ice in the glasses and, until recently at least, the smell of pipes or cigars. Usually, the sleeping quarters are more spartan, resembling more a boys' school dorm than a luxury suite, but if you sniff closely, you can catch the most familiar smell in clubdom, Pears Soap. The tackle room will be neat, with lockers, and will have a stove for drying wet gear. Rod racks are on the walls outside the screened verandah, and there will be wooden chairs of the kind known generally as Adirondacks, though in our part of the country we call them Gatineau Drinking Chairs.

Since Americans built so many of these places, it follows there must be similar buildings on lakes and streams in the United States, and one is told they are even more palatial, and more imitative of the hunting and fishing lodges built by European nobility. Few Canadians have have visited these places, partly for the simple reason that the fish and game are more plentiful here, above all the Atlantic salmon.

In the Canadian case, the atmosphere is of woodsmoke, pine-scented luxury, with an edge of excitement from the

prospect of the fishing, and an element of danger that comes from being in the bush, on rivers that can drown you, and where forests abound with bears that can eat you. For the club hand, it is heaven—for the first-time visitor, it can be inhibiting, and the urge to "do the right thing" can spoil the fun.

Simon Reisman would fish the Sainte-Marguerite for the next twenty years, and it would become for him what the Old Fort is for me—the favorite river. And for all the memories he has of it, and of the guides, and the anglers he has fished it with, he remembers that first time with an emotion that borders on wonder. How could anybody be so lucky? He still marvels at it.

That first trip, the limit was four salmon a day, and Simon soon found that, if he worked at it, he could get his four. He was shown how by his appointed guide, Leon Dupres, and the first two fish were hooked by this veteran riverman, who handed the rod to Reisman as soon as the salmon was on. "He showed me what to do, and I did it," Simon recalls, "and each of those fish was over twenty pounds. At lunchtime I worked on my casting and had a good take, and brought him in, and I did the whole thing myself in ten minutes. That fish was sixteen pounds, and right after lunch we were into another at the Traverse Pool. Funny thing, in all my years on the Sainte-Marguerite I've never had another fish out of that pool." Simon says he wasn't a natural fly fisherman, and could never get the finesse of the "poetry-in-motion" casters. "But I can now do it quite well—I work very hard at it, and don't goof off or turn the rod over to the guide." Strikes occur, he says, in direct relation to the amount of time the fly is in the water.

At the end of that first week of fishing, the salmon were packed in wooden coffins with ice and snow, and shipped to the homes of the six guest anglers. Simon recalls how the catch arrived.

He was in his Department of Finance office when his wife, Connie, phoned to say the fish had arrived. Each fishermen was permitted to take home eight fish, of the eighteen each had caught—the rest were distributed locally.

Simon had told Connie, when he arrived from the trip, that "This was the most exciting thing I ever did in my life," and the remark had not gone down well. In fact, she said, "Drop dead!" Now, he told her to clean the fish, provoking a long silence on the phone.

She said there were eight boxes in the driveway, and she couldn't even lift them. With the packing, each box weighed forty to fifty pounds, for a total of almost a quarter of a ton.

"There was only one fish store in town," says Simon, "Lapointe's in the Market. So I phoned them and told my story, and said the fish would be lost if they couldn't help me. They finally agreed to rent me a locker, and came out and picked up the fish and put them in with my name on them. For years after that, I always had a locker at Lapointe's and it always had fish in it—when the fishing got poorer and the catches went down our home freezer was enough, so we dropped the locker. But from 1954 to now we've never been without a supply of salmon—the ones in the freezer now are from last summer's trip to the Jupiter. And I've got two invitations to fish this summer."

TEACHING THE YANKS

Simon gets touchy when it is suggested that the Yanks took him and Canada to the cleaners in the free trade negotiations, and when he gets on the subject he talks of nothing else, and will go into chapter and verse about the trade agreement, with all the clauses and sub-clauses. I have to cut him off and tell him that is another book. This one is about Simon the fisherman, and we haven't time or room for free trade, though it may sneak in from time to time in conversation. Simon might write a book about it himself, though he says he can't afford the time. During one of our

gabfests, he took a phone call from a TV reporter who had some questions about the cultural side of free trade and, by the time Simon had set her straight, he was so steamed I couldn't get him back to earth or, to be more precise, to water. No Yankee negotiator had ever got the best of him, at the table or anywhere else, so I saw my opening and asked him if he had ever learned anything from those master anglers from the States. And out came the story of how Simon introduced Canadian-style fly fishing for salmon to the farthest reaches of Alaska, and started a new sports industry beyond the Aleutians, in the inlet of the Bering Sea that is known as Bristol Bay.

It all happened because Simon was a director of Nelson Brothers, a subsidiary of British Columbia Packers, and he persuaded the Nelbro board to hold its annual meeting where the fish were, taking care to pack his rod, reel, flies and waders for the trip, even though he had been told there would be no call for sissy Eastern gear, and the more rugged stuff needed for the Alaska Big Ones would be provided on the scene.

To get there, you fly to Anchorage and take a plane southwest to Dillingham, and then a float plane to the village of King Salmon on the Naknek River. For once, Simon saw enough fish to satisfy his wildest dreams.

It was July 1, the heart of the fishing season, though the American hosts were more inclined to associate the date with the Fourth of July. It turned out to be the biggest year in the long history of the Bristol Bay fishery, even though the fishermen went on strike and cut down the catch. Sixty-four million fish came into Bristol Bay that week, and they caught and processed twenty million of them. Simon was goggled-eyed and twitchy to get fishing on waters that held that many fish, wanting to throw off his director's hat and put on his fishing cap.

"Let's get fishing," he said, and they did.

The Naknek has a population of native rainbow trout, running up to thirty pounds trophy size, with a general run of around ten to fifteen pounds. They introduced Simon to an outfitter named Colonel Woods, a veteran of the United States Air Force, who was immediately sized up by Simon as a meat fisherman, interested in trophies as a routine—trolling for King Salmon in the morning and for the rainbow trout in the afternoon, using heavy spinning gear, everything under the direction of the boss. The idea was not so much enjoyment as the catching of fish, and the first morning Simon got his big one, which, as he recalls, was "like bringing a horse into the boat." It weighed fifty-one pounds! As became a visiting director's fish, Simon's was cut up into fillets, and they shipped the whole thing home to Ottawa. As Simon says, when Pacific salmon are from cold waters and treated right, "you can't do much better."

That afternoon, they went trolling for rainbows, and "Woodsy" knew exactly what everybody had to do, which is not the way to make Simon Reisman happy. He got bored, in fact, and his bottom got numb sitting in the boat.

Fly fishing was mentioned, but the host didn't show any interest, calling it a waste of time.

Late in the afternoon, they were trolling past what Simon thought, with his pride in being able to "read" the waters, was a perfect pool. There was a bit of a sand bar, a riffle of water, a bit of a run above, and "it just seemed right."

"Drop me off here," said Simon.

"You'll be wasting your time," said Woodsy.

"Look," said Simon, "let me waste my time."

So they dumped him out on his sand bar and left him alone, and he started to play the pool, and nothing happened.

He fished it with a Jock Scott, and changed flies three times, and nothing. Finally, he put on a fly known as the Black Bear, a hair fly on a Number Six hook with a long shank, with silver winding, and bear hair like an umbrella on the top.

On the third cast, a lovely fish took, a nine-pound rainbow that ran out and leaped as a rainbow should. Simon brought it in and killed it, and tied it onto a piece of green nylon cord, which he affixed to a bush. Half a dozen casts later, he was into another fish—but this time it wasn't a rainbow, it was a sockeye salmon. Woodsy had said the sockeye never take a fly, so Simon relished this one especially.

An hour and a half later, the guide and boat returned from their trolling and asked if Simon had had any luck.

"I held up one of the fish."

"What is that?"

"A sockeye."

"On the fly?"

"Yes, on the fly."

He asked if Simon had any others.

"So," Simon recalls, "I held up another one, and then a third. By this time I had seven fish—two were rainbows, and five were sockeyes. There was no limit to the sockeyes, and all on the same fly, and all within twenty or twenty-five yards. Remember, he had said sockeye never take a fly, and the rainbows thereabouts, rarely."

"Holy Jeez," said Woodsy.

The next day, Simon went back to the same spot and took another heavy catch on the fly, culminating at day's end with what our hero calls "a very good rainbow."

"I am sure it was a trophy," he recalls. "He took my whole line out, and he was into the backing four or five times. Each time I started to get him in, he went again, and finally he just made a run for the sea, and I tightened my reel as much as I dared tighten it, I didn't dare tighten it any more. And he just took out the line, and then he took out the backing, and there I was, and it snapped, right where the backing was attached to the reel, and it was over. He was a magnificent fish, he really was—he jumped three or four times."

"Did you try to go with him?"

"There was no way to go with him. The boat left us there. The only thing would have been to swim, and I've never done that."

"What did you do with runaway fish?"

"Well, that same thing happened to me only one other time, on a much smaller fish, on the Jupiter, on the Sea Pool. The Sea Pool is where the fresh fish have just come in, and they're wonderful. They've got the sea lice on them and they're tough, and I got into a good-sized fish and played him, about ten or twelve pounds, and I followed him down as far as I could until I couldn't follow him any more. So all I was left with was either virtually lock the reel or let him run. So he ran and I lost the whole thing again—lost it, he took it all the way to the sea with him, and he's gone. And I was left there with nothing but rod and bare reel, nothing else."

It struck me, out of that story from Alaska, that Simon might have come out on the short end, because of the runaway rainbow, except that Simon found out later that his example brought about a change on the Naknek River, and that Woodsy now has a couple of boats devoted entirely to fly fishing, as taught by our boardroom boy from the eastern waters.

Simon got a kick out of teaching the Yanks new tricks, and also getting one up on that bane of all anglers, the tyrannical guide.

"Don't get me wrong," says Simon, "I get on well with most salmon guides—I pay a lot of attention to these guys, it's their river, and their profession.

"Except," he said, starting to sound like my father, "that on some of those New Brunswick rivers, the Scottish and Irish guides have very little respect for fishermen. In fact, they don't really like them and refer to them as 'sports,' and talk about 'my sport' and 'your sport' and they make fun of them behind their backs, and sometimes to their faces. It's only the odd fisherman that will win their respect."

And I got the feeling that Simon felt himself to be among that chosen few, or at least hoped he was.

JULIA CATCHES ONE

We were working on a bottle of Glen Morangue, which I had provided to get Simon into a midwinter angling mood, there being none of his favorite Polish vodka in the Québec grog shop. There was lots of Geneva gin, that favorite of Quebeckers indoors and out, though I have yet to meet anyone of other extractions who likes it, including the Dutch, who distill it for the Québec market, the way the Japanese make those plastic muskies for Canadian mantles.

"Simon," I said, "you talk mostly about the Sainte-Marguerite, the Sand Hill and the Jupiter, and yet you have fished that greatest of rivers, the Grand Cascapedia, and you hardly talk about it at all."

He frowned. "Who says it's the greatest?"

"Shirley Woods."

"How many rivers has he fished?"

"He says he's fished thirty-five rivers in forty years."

"And he says the Grand Cascapedia is the best?"

"Well, what he says is that, over the years, it has been the most consistent producer of the largest Atlantic salmon in North America."

"Well, maybe. Size isn't everything."

I knew Simon had fished the Grand Cascapedia, because it was on his list, and besides, Bill Fox, who was once Brian Mulroney's press secretary, told me he had been on that river with Simon, as guests of Frank Moores, the consultant's consultant and the man who, as premier of Newfoundland, had sustained the helicopter industry to get him and his parents to the province's salmon pools.

Moores is recalled as Joey Smallwood's successor as Newfoundland premier, the man who promised a royal commission into Joey's regime. It was never held. When Brian Peckford succeeded Moores and promised to investigate his predecessor, that, too, fell upon the rocks. And when Peckford was replaced by Clyde Wells, it was thought there would be a probe into Peckford, but it didn't happen.

Moores has prospered and now controls the finest water on the Grand Cascapedia, and is described as a man who lives for salmon. But I couldn't get Simon to talk much about him, or the river.

"I suppose," he said, "Shirley Woods caught a trophy fish on the river and that's why he says it's the best."

"No," I said, swirling my horn of single malt, "but his daughter did, and she made the cover of the *Anglers' Club of New York Bulletin* with a picture of it."

Simon whistled, and said he had heard that, at one time, five Rockefellers belonged to that prestigious club. He knew, too, that Shirley Woods fished in the best company, and had written some of the best books ever turned out in Canada on hunting and fishing, besides being a stockbroker of note and one of the best fly tyers in the land.

I showed Simon a handful of flies Shirley had tied for me, including one called the Black Coltrin, named after the street in Ottawa where Woods had lived for years, before pulling stakes for Mahone Bay, the prettiest town in Nova Scotia.

"That's the fly she had on," I said. "The only fly she ever fished with."

Simon raised his bushy brows.

"Of course," I added, "she only fished one day in her life."

I had his interest now, and so unfolded the story of Julia Woods, nineteen, and the biggest salmon, as told to me by her father.

It was a June Sunday, and Shirley had invited his daughter for a day's fishing on the Grand Cascapedia, he himself having fished the river for a week without result. He had wangled an invitation to fish that Sunday on some storied water upriver from the stretch he had been fishing, so he picked Julia up at the Bonaventure airport and they headed upriver.

They walked into Fraser's Pool, a bottle-shaped stretch with a lovely stone bottom and a steady flow of green water, and Shirley proceeded to show his daughter the rudiments of fly casting, she having never had a fly rod in her hand before.

He started her at the main part of the pool, taking a step downstream after each cast, while he watched from the bank above. Suddenly he saw a huge grey-green shape rise to her fly and then disappear. The salmon didn't touch the fly and Julia didn't see it, so he immediately told Julia to bring in her line, meanwhile skidding down the bank and placing a piece of wood on the gravel opposite where he had seen the fish.

"This guy really knows his stuff," said Simon, admiringly.

"Yes," I said, "but wait till you hear the rest."

"Pour me another."

I did, and went on with the story.

Julia was instructed to back up about six paces, and fish down again with exactly the same length of line—about twenty-five feet. The fish had moved for a Number 2 Skunk, but refused a Number 2 Silver Rat and then a Number 2 Rusty Rat—Shirley always uses the word *refused* for a fish that doesn't take, indicating that acceptance can be obtained if you do it right.

He changed Julia's fly once more to the Number 2 Black Coltrin, which he describes as black fisher tail wing, black mohair body ribbed with silver, jungle cock cheeks and golden pheasant tail.

This time, when the Black Coltrin passed over the salmon, the fish engulfed the fly. Julia coolly set the hook and joined the battle with what her father describes as a hell of a big fish, and he has handled his share of monsters.

He was worried that, if it chose to leave the pool, they would lose it in the quarter-mile of heavy rapids immediately below—if it wanted to go, there was no way to hold it. But the fish proved very docile and Julia kept it on a short line. Even so, it was slowly drifting down the pool toward the rapids, so father decided he would wade out into the foot of the pool into swift but shallow water, and try to make enough commotion to scare the fish upstream. The fish was co-operating nicely, not more than twenty feet above him and about the same distance from the bank.

At this point it is useful to note that Shirley Woods, like his brother John and father Shirley before him, dresses impeccably for the sport, and cuts a figure with rod or gun that would do credit to the grand days of Abercombie & Fitch, not to mention the garb they designed themselves for the family outdoors outfitting business.

"You get the picture," I told Simon.

"I get it. I've seen the Woods boys in action."

Quietly, Shirley laid the huge rim of the net on the gravel bottom and told Julia to gently lead the fish over the net, like a dog on a leash, which she proceeded to do.

Shirley says now he knew he was doing a dumb thing, since the fish was too green to net, and you never, ever net a big fish from the tail. He wasn't even sure the net was big enough.

But he desperately wanted to avoid a long fight for Julia, and the fish looked so magnificent in the clear water, with its black back as broad as the blade of a paddle—he could literally see every scale on the silver sides. For Shirley, the whole thing had a dreamlike quality until he lifted the net.

(Simon gulped, and beckoned for a refill.)

At this point, the salmon exploded into action, and instead of breaking outside Shirley to open water, it thrashed out of the net and landed between him and the bank. The monofilament leader, twenty-pound test, went around Shirley's neck and threatened to throttle him as the fish tightened the loop, but luckily for father the line snapped in a second, and away went the mighty salmon.

Shirley Woods, though generous to a fault, is not a man given to humility, but he says he was mortified at his stupidity. Sloshing to the bank, he flung down the net and beat the ground with his fists, while contemplating a rending of his expensive garments, and uttering cries of anguish.

"I have seen Shirley in this state myself," I commented, "in the billiard room of the old Rideau Club, after missing a shot. He puts on quite a show, and has been known to snap a billiard cue with his bare hands."

He was aware of the fact that only seven salmon had been caught on the entire Grand Cascapedia to that date, but Julia was unruffled.

"Don't worry about that, Dad," she said. "We'll just put on another Black Coltrin and catch another one."

Shirley did as she suggested with a heavy heart, knowing the odds. He had fished the whole previous week without so much as a rise.

But ten minutes later, she was into another monster.

This one jumped repeatedly, and then headed down the rapids, with Julia slipping and sliding over the stones in pursuit, and father following after with a fine disregard for the icy water, the perils of the rapids, or the crease in his pants. He waded in up to his chest, and took the rod around one big boulder, while tripping on some roots. Julia, rod in hand, climbed over fallen spruce trees that lay across the river. The word went out on the jungle telegraph that a big fish was being played, and two river wardens, the head guide of Tracadie camp and the Woods's host, Bud Campbell, materialized out of the bush and were following along—all five experienced anglers giving Julia the benefit of their advice, and she ignoring them all.

There were a lot of close calls, but she played the fish beautifully. Once, the line got tangled in the handle of the Bogdan reel and the fish chose that moment to jump, with the line jammed tight. Finally, they reached a quiet stretch of water below the rapids, known as Lazy Bogan, and Julia was descending from the shallow bank to the pool, when a tiny leopard frog jumped in front of her and she shied back, whipping the rod in an arc above her head. Nothing snapped.

Julia and Shirley waded out, side by side, into Lazy Bogan, and she started to pump and reel the fish in. Father stood like a heron, poised with the net, determined not to screw it up again.

The fish came in nicely, looking like a torpedo in the crystal water, and when Julia caught full sight of it, she became transfixed and stopped reeling. Shirley cajoled her into bringing it all the way in, and she swung it into the mouth of the net like an old pro. Shirley describes the action.

"I scooped the fish and the brand-new net crumpled like a piece of spaghetti. So I grabbed the rim, the fish being well and truly in the bag, and manhandled it to shore and fell upon it with a shriek of triumph, which was echoed by the gallery."

Two of them carried the big fish the half-mile back to the car, and when they got back to camp they weighed it—forty-two pounds, the biggest salmon caught on the river that season.

Shirley recalls that, when he scooped the fish, the hook fell out as soon as it was in the net. Only one of the twin barbs of the heavy Mustad double hook had actually held the fish, and it was completely sprung, and nearly straight.

"I've only seen a hook bent on a fish once," I told Simon, "when Esmond Butler was fishing for piranha during the Governor General's visit to Guyana. Esmond didn't keep any fish, but he kept that hook as Exhibit A."

As for Julia's salmon, Shirley traced the outline of it and had its silhouette carved in butternut, and it hangs in his study with a plaque giving credit to the woman who caught it.

Julia hasn't been salmon fishing since, saying, "What would I do for an encore?"

Shirley agrees, adding that reflected glory is better than none.

"And that," said Simon admiringly, "is a hell of a story. Now let me tell you about the Sand Hill..."

BUY ME
A RIVER

Ottawa has sent many weird and wonderful deputations out into the land, but none stranger than the passle of senior mandarins who set out in an old fishing boat to reclaim the Labrador salmon rivers from the Americans, who had appropriated the best fly fishing in the world as an add-on to the bases they got from Winston Churchill, in return for Franklin Roosevelt's forty old destroyers from the First World War.

The bases-for-rust-buckets deal didn't mention the fishing, of course, but no sooner were the Yanks established in the old colony of

Newfoundland and Labrador than they were seeking out the best pools and throwing up lodgings on the riverbanks, along with clearings where the helicopters could fly in from places like Gander and Goose Bay and Stephenville.

The effort to recapture those treasured waters continues to this day, but the story really begins with those mandarins in their pea-green boat, working their way along the Labrador coast, disguised as a Small Harbor Inspection Team, but with weapons at the ready, in the form of fly rods, waders, nets and bug repellant.

I have seen authority take strange forms, as when a party of American canoeists, camped by remote Wilberforce Falls on the Hood River, had a visit from our party of fishermen, which included the U.S. Ambassador to Canada, who sought assurance that his countrymen were being well treated. Since the only live things sharing that part of the vast northern landscape were the local musk oxen, the canoeists reported the Canadian hospitality was great.

And then there was Dimche Belovsky, the best-remembered of all the congenial Yugoslav ambassadors to Canada, who flew to Dawson City as part of an ambassadorial tour of the North sponsored by the Canadian government, only to find, on landing in the Yukon River, that there was no Canadian official on board.

Belovsky, as the senior person in the delegation, assumed command, accepted the welcome of the crowd of citizens on the dock, and proceeded to hear their grievances against their government, which they had taken the trouble to inscribe in a lengthy document. Belovsky carried the document back to Whitehorse and, at a formal banquet that night, read out to the Canadian Northern Affairs minister the list of his taxpayers' grievances.

I recall the time Governor General Ed Schreyer was touring the Arctic, with former Territories' Commissioner Stu Hodgson arriving ahead of him at Bathurst Inlet Lodge. The local Inuit assumed Hodgson *was* the Governor General, since they had been accustomed to look on him as their emperor, so they put on their drum and dance act for him and went home. They were bewildered to be rounded up the next night, to repeat the show for a total stranger by the name of Schreyer.

Natives of High River, Alberta, used to be amused by the sight of local native Joe Clark, then Prime Minister of Canada, sporting a tractor hat, at the wheel of his mother's rusty old half-ton truck, the incongruous part being the RCMP squad cars running shotgun, front and rear, weapons at the ready.

Picture, then, these mandarins on their fishing boat, led by John McDonald, the Deputy Minister of Public Works; Jack "Jake" Warren, Deputy Minister of Industry, Trade and Commerce, future High Commissioner to the United Kingdom and Ambassador to the United States; Edgar Ritchie, Under-Secretary for External Affairs and future Ambassador to the United States and Ireland, and our man, Simon Reisman, then Deputy Minister of Finance and future Trade Ambassador. Tom Whelan, master angler and Newfoundland agent for Public Works, was along to give expert guidance.

Oh, yes, and Douglas Fullerton, he of the most celebrated stammer in Canadian public life, who, while he would not share ambassadorial rank with his companions, was a big wheel in the Canada Council and would later win for the national capital its network of ski trails, cycle paths and the longest skating rink in the world.

It would be safe to say that never had so much bureaucratic clout been assembled on a small Newfoundland inshore fishing vessel, and if they had chosen to wear their Homburg hats, then the symbol of their rank, the party would have taken on a distinctly funereal air.

Instead of which, they were in a festive mood, tasting the adventure of pretending to chart the harbors, while casting their flies in uncharted waters, unknown at least to Canadian anglers.

They knew about the mightiest of the salmon rivers, the Eagle, well-named after the national bird of the U.S.A., and a virtual American waterway because of its proximity to Goose Bay. Senior Canadian military officers had been known to fish the Eagle as guests of their American allies. The Canadian brass had even reached the point of pitching tents on the Eagle and inviting defence contractors to fish there, and even Canadian politicians who might be appreciative of a little TLC from the defence establishment.

Our party of mandarins sniffed in and out of the mouths of smaller rivers, like the Big Bear and the Little Bear, and some that had no names on the map, working their way toward what would be, for most, the Shangri La of salmon rivers, the Sand Hill.

The United States Air Force had been established on the Sand Hill ever since 1943, when it was known as the Army Air Corps, and the maps even noted a place on the river known as Chopper Point, because that was where the helicopters landed, near the base camp for the fishing.

It was with beating hearts that the crew of the little fishing boat nosed in past the promontory known as Indian Tickle, and saw, for the first time, the mouth of the Sand Hill River.

The boat's dory took them ashore and they sized up the stream, trying to figure where the first of the salmon pools might be—salmon they knew were there, because there had been tales of fabulous catches on the river, in numbers, if not in size.

Jake Warren, described by Reisman as the most stylish fisherman he ever knew—"I kid him about caring more for the style of fishing than the substance, and he takes it as a compliment"—was the first to fish, electing to work the first pool into the wind. Those who saw what happened remain impressed to this day, for a gust of wind caught Warren's fly in the air and carried it back toward him. Warren has a habit of opening his mouth when he casts, and the fly went straight in and lodged itself firmly on the inside of his cheek.

Now, if you have ever had a fishhook imbedded in any part of your clothing, let alone on your anatomy, you will know the problem it represents, and the more you fiddle with it, the worse it gets, since that's what hooks are designed to do to fish. In Warren's case, though, his reaction was swift, and brutal. He put his hand in his mouth, grasped the hook, and tore it out with a single yank, spitting out a gob of blood in the process. Then he went on fishing. Later, his only comment was that any wound in the mouth heals, with the help of a little whisky.

Ed Ritchie was next to get his line into the water, and as luck would have it, he hooked the first salmon of the expedition on the Black Bear River. Trouble was, while Ritchie was an experienced trout fisherman, he had never had a salmon before, and when the fish made its first run and jump, he froze. It was as though he had turned to marble, holding the rod rigidly and showing no reaction to the antics of the fish, which were spectacular. Three runs, three jumps, and it was over, leaving Canada's leading diplomat with a limp line and a mumbled expression of apologies to his fellows, saying he had no idea anything so violent could happen in such a peaceful place. Ritchie, best known as the Canadian diplomat most like Lester Pearson, got the hang of it later, though, like Pearson, he never did become obsessed with the sport the way Warren and Reisman did.

On their way back downstream from that first foray, the party got divided and there ensued what came to be known as Jake Warren's Epic Swim, the deputy minister having decided to cross from one side of the river to the other for better footing, thinking the river was shallow enough for a wade. It wasn't. He went up to his knees, then to his hips, then to his chest, and then he was afloat—hip waders, backpack, rod and all. Nothing daunted, he struck out for the far shore, managing to handle hip boots, pack and rod in the process, without uttering so much as a cry. Those who saw it said it beat the famous photograph of angling guru Lee Wulff, diving off a Newfoundland bridge in his chest waders to prove a submerged fisherman could survive (a lot have not, including a couple of good friends.)

Warren made it with everything intact, except for his dignity, which for once was ruffled, and he admitted he was cold, proceeding downstream at a trot to restore his circulation, having asked one of his fellows to carry the salmon he had stuffed into one of the deep pockets of his jacket. It was the only fish caught that day, and they dined on it that night aboard ship.

The dory that was supposed to pick the party up at the mouth of the Sand Hill was not there when they arrived, but an Inuit fisherman was there, and agreed to ferry them to their boat, for a fee of two bottles of rum.

At the end of three days of fishing the Sand Hill, our mandarins had had enough, and while they were waiting for a float plane to ferry them to Goose Bay, they ventured onto an iceberg that was floating by, and collected buckets of ice for their fish, and their drinks. Then they went ashore to investigate a small cemetery, Reisman taking along a rod, as was his custom. This time, though, it was a spinning rod, and as soon as he was on the rocky shore, he started casting into the salt water. In came a six-pound Arctic char, then another, and another, followed by several sea trout. Simon put the fish into a pool in the granite rock and, when his fellows came back from the cemetery, he showed them his catch—more fish than they had caught in the previous week of fishing. The rest swarmed back to the boat for their rods and returned to join the sport, and by late afternoon they had char galore.

When they got back to their boat, a Newfoundland cod-fishing boat anchored nearby for a Sunday rest, and two of them rowed over in a dory.

"Wuz you fishin' dere?" they asked.

"Yes."

"Didja get enny?"

"Quite a lot." And the catch was put on display.

"Wotja git 'em wit'?"

The lures were displayed, and rum was poured.

"You got dose fish wit' dose?"

"Yes."

"Kin we buy 'em of yez?"

No need, said Simon, giving them his whole box of lures and wishing them good luck.

"Kin we give yez anything?" they asked.

"Well," said Simon, "we're a little short of salmon to take home, and we were wondering if you had caught any."

"Well," they said, "we've been fishing for cod, but we got a few salmon, too."

Turned out they had two, averaging about fourteen pounds, and they would be perfect for our heroes to take home.

"I remember the fisherman who was wearing glasses," says Simon. "He didn't look like all that much of a fisherman, he looked more like a schoolteacher. He was the one who was doing the talking."

"I can't sell them to you," he said.

"Why can't you?"

"Cause we need them for tickets."

"Tickets?"

"Yes. We have to have so many before we have a claim for unemployment. It's based on the fish we land, and salmon are the best for the tickets."

"What are these tickets worth to you?" asked Reisman. He pressed his luck. "You'll go out and you'll get more salmon, eh? We're headed home to Ottawa, and there aren't any salmon there."

The bespectacled fisherman paused, said to wait a minute, and sat down and started to figure out entitlements.

Finally, he said, "These tickets are worth about eight dollars each."

"So, what do you want for your fish?"

"Eight dollars, plus."

"Plus what?"

"Give me twenty dollars for the pair."

So they did, and threw in a small bottle of rum, and they were happy, and our mandarins had two good fish.

The plane never did arrive that afternoon, so the decision was made to eat the two salmon, which the cook on board offered to prepare in the Newfoundland fashion—cut into chunks and boiled, with an onion and some fatback in the pot. The whole process takes twenty minutes, and Simon says you can have all your fancy ways of baking, poaching and dressing up that greatest of fish for catching or eating, nothing ever tasted better. A helluva way to take care of unemployment insurance, is how he puts it.

The plane came the next day, in time to get our mandarins to Goose Bay just before darkness set in, and bureaucratic minds shifted into their normal gears, leading to a call to the Canadian base commander, a staff car pickup, lodging in a woman's residence that was empty for the summer, including hot water and everything needed to restore our heroes to Ottawa standard for the flight home.

One thing the participants recall is that they scarcely talked shop at all during the adventure. They were easy in each other's company—"All of us were pretty expert at something," Reisman recalls, "and we were all pretty close. We talked about Labrador and the outports, about fishing. What do you talk about on a river? You do not talk shop."

And they discussed how nice it would be to own something on the Sand Hill. Reisman couldn't do without it. Through Toronto investment friends, he heard that the Americans who had the lease of the river were looking for a couple of "tame Canadians," who would let the Americans continue to have the run of the river without the danger of losing their lease. That very fall, Reisman and his fellow deputy minister, Jim Grandy, anted up two thousand dollars each by way of subscription, which entitled them to two weeks of fishing a year, with the privilege of inviting guests.

From then on, the Sand Hill was Simon's sure thing, the embellishments being other rivers where he was invited to fish. To the Sand Hill went Jake Warren, and military officers, and the fastidious Esmond Butler, secretary to successive Governors General, who came to regard the Sand Hill as heaven.

Ten years ago, Simon was plagued by a wonky knee and felt he could no longer go to the river, so he made a present of his position on the water to Jake Warren.

"Then," says Reisman with a chuckle, "I got the knee operated on and got fixed up as good as new, and from then on I've been going to the Sand Hill as Jake's guest, on what used to be my own water!"

He bared the knee and described his upper tibia osteomety, "a rebuilding, re-jigging, cutting in there and around, you can see the shape of it. They chop it, and they have to use chisels and hammers and saws, and they rebuild it and put a wedge in. It's gone now again and I'll have to replace it with a plastic knee, but it's lasted through ten years of fishing, and last year I was skiing."

The lease on the Sand Hill has since been turned over to an outfitter, named Bill Bennett, who gives special privileges to the founders of the club, including Americans and Canadians, and Simon's trip to the river last year cost him more than $5,000, not bad as salmon fishing trips go, when you figure in the transportation.

Still, there is guide Homan Campbell, Simon's nomination for the greatest guide of his experience—part Inuit, part Indian and part Scot, who "lumbers like a bear and looks like a pear."

Homan is a man of few words and fewer choices of fly, favoring one that is small, and black, and lightly dressed with a strand of silver on the shank. Simon's biggest argument with Homan was over a knot called a Newfie Hitch, or more politely a Portland Hitch, consisting of a simple loop that is passed over the eye of the fly, on top of the knot, giving the fly a cockeyed posture on the water, swimming sideways.

Simon was fishing without the hitch, and Homan objected.

"You don't have the hitch on."

"Well, I don't like the hitch on it. I don't think the fly sits right with the hitch."

"Well, you won't get them without the hitch."

"Okay."

The hitch was put on.

Simon fished the fly out into the pool, and soon was into the biggest salmon he had ever seen on the Sand Hill. At least fourteen pounds. But he lost it.

"Homan," said Simon, "I can never hold my goddam salmon when I take them on the Newfie Hitch. I don't think they take very well."

Homan grunted, and said that, when the water is the color of tea, as it often is in Labrador, the fish can see a hitched fly better than one fished straight, and the fisherman can see the wake of it better, too.

"I lost it, Homan."

"Yeah," he replied "but you'd never have gotten it without the hitch. I know these fish."

"I've caught a lot of fish without it."

"Yeah, but they were mostly grilse, weren't they?"

Simon agreed.

"You'll attract more fish with the hitch," said Homan.

"Yes, and I'll hold more fish without it."

And there the matter rests, a stalemate impossible of solution.

Simon's favorite story of Homan Campbell came from last year's trip, when, bad knee and all, he elected to hike the five kilometers over rough tundra to the best upstream pools on the Sand Hill.

No sooner had they arrived than Simon was into a good-sized fish, and suddenly there was a crack like a rifle shot, and his rod broke in two, leaving him with just the butt and a short length of graphite below the break. He fought the fish bare-handed and landed it and killed it, and that seemed to be the end of his fishing for the day.

But something came to him from his boyhood experiences with alder, so he went and cut himself a stout branch. From it, he fashioned two splints, and he fastened the rod together with adhesive tape he had in his pack. Within an hour, he was able to start fishing again. Homan had watched the entire operation without comment, and when the rod was back in action he asked to see the splint, and he pronounced it good.

"I think he was impressed that a city slicker would even try such a thing," says Simon. "Anyway, he treated me like a brother and later, when I was dragging behind because of my knee, I came upon Homan sitting on a rock, and he pointed out into the water and said there was a salmon there."

Homan said he knew the fish was there because he passed a fly over him and raised him, and then rested him until Simon came along. Simon put his fly where Homan told him to, and the salmon came and the rod held up and it was the best catch of the day.

Simon still has the splinted rod among his fishing gear, though he never used it again.

FEELING HORNY

B ack to Reisman the negotiator for a moment, as he tells it.

> You know that I did the aboriginal land claims agreement in 1982 and 1983, and it was passed and proclaimed on the last day that Pierre Trudeau was in office; June 30, 1984.
>   I negotiated that agreement, and it is the only aboriginal land claim agreement North of Sixty that was completed, and made the law of the land. And I not only negotiated this, but, because I

was reasonably well-known to people like Allan MacEachen and Pierre Trudeau and some of the other government people, I was able to persuade them to do it.

By *do it*, I mean we completed it, we signed an agreement. It needed legislation, it needed priority, and we were able to do it, because we were able to persuade Pierre Trudeau that this was a worthwhile thing to do. It was proclaimed on the last day he was in office, and in conversation Allan asked if this was going to solve the problem.

I said "No, but it'll get them off your backs. They want this, they need this."

"You recommend it?"

"Yes, I do. You won't get a better agreement."

And I added, to the prime minister, "Pierre, there are a lot of things for which you will not be remembered. But for certain you'll be remembered for this one."

"You think so?"

"Yes. It won't get you in any trouble, it's a worthwhile thing to do, and it will be part of your contribution to Canadian history."

When Simon was in the Arctic on this job, whenever he could, he would want to fish. Trouble was, he didn't have very good luck.

I got some in little lakes, but that's not what I wanted. I wanted some real good char fishing, and it didn't happen.

At Saks Harbour, the Inuit promised me good fishing, but it was not successful. They got me into the boat, but the tides weren't right and I never did get to fish. I heard a lot about how one of our party, an old man, was on the trek that brought the herd of reindeer across the ice bridge from Siberia in the early '30s, to start a new industry to provide meat, and how it wound up providing ground-up reindeer antlers to be sold in the Far East as aphrodisiacs. But no fish.

The trouble with those reindeer, I gather, was that they didn't want to come, and every year they wanted to turn around and head for home, which is why it took six or seven years to get them settled in our territory. It was a great story, but it didn't help the fishing.

That reindeer herd almost wrecked Reisman's negotiation, because the owner of the herd claimed he owned the land the reindeer were grazing on. "We finally got across the idea that the deer had the right to pasture, but that the land reverted to the Inuit."

TOO GOOD
FISHING

"Have you ever," I asked Simon, one afternoon at the Club, "been embarrassed by too much good fishing?"

"Have I ever!" Simon took the bait.

The occasion was on the Eagle River in Labrador, where the armed forces encampment has hosted the greats of governments, armies and air forces ever since the Second World War. For three weeks every year, a tent encampment springs up on the banks of the Eagle, ostensibly as an extension of the Search and Rescue operation based at Goose Bay. The campsite happens to be adjacent to some of the best salmon fishing anywhere, but, as part of their "dues," guests are expected to take part in lectures and demonstrations on survival in the Canadian bush.

So you don't so much *go* to camp on the Eagle, you *attend* it, and as Deputy Minister of Finance, Simon Reisman was regularly invited to three days on the Eagle, ferried in by helicopter from Goose Bay and living under canvas while on the river.

Some summers, the guest of honor was Governor General Roland Michener who, like his principal secretary, Esmond Butler, was a keen angler, and took salmon fishing as seriously as any of his predecessors as commander-in-chief.

Fishing on the Eagle is from canoes, except for one larger wooden boat, owned by guide Bill Brown, which is known as *The Queen Mary*, and is placed at the Governor General's disposal whenever he is in camp. It was Michener's custom to invite each of his fellow guests to fish with him during the nine turns every angler got, over the three days, and when Simon got his invitation he was honored, because he was a fan of Michener's, both as GG and as a fisherman.

Michener invited Simon to sit in the bow, which was the preferred position, and no sooner had they reached the first pool, the one called Governor's Rock, than Simon was into a fish.

When there are two anglers in a boat and one has a fish on, the other reels in and waits until the fight is over, before casting again. The Governor General obliged, and Simon brought his salmon to boat as quickly as he could, after which he offered to change places with Michener, giving the Gov the preferred position.

But Michener told Simon to stay where he was, a variation on the old Newfoundland saying of "stay where yer at and I'll come where yer to." Both men resumed casting and, in two minutes, Simon was into another fish. Michener reeled in and waited while the fish was fought and brought to net.

"Roly," said Simon, before biting his tongue at such undue familiarity, and trying to remember what to call the Governor General, mentally rejecting Your Highness, Your Grace and Your Majesty, finally settling for plain *sir*.

"Sir," he said, "you must come forward. I insist."

"My dear fellow," said Michener, "I am quite content—fish on."

Fish on, was right. In about five minutes, a fish was on, and again the Governor General reeled in and sat quietly while Reisman, flushed with embarrassment, brought that fish in, unable to shake it loose no matter how hard he tried.

It was turning into a great morning for Reisman, but a dull one for Michener, and still the GG would not accept Reisman's offer of the forward position.

Guide Bill Brown came to the rescue by suggesting they move to the next pool, known as the Sand Bar, and as soon as they got there and Bill turned off the motor, Reisman asked to be put ashore so he could fish from the beach.

"I didn't like to leave His Excellency," said Simon, finally thinking of the right vice-regal label, "but I was too embarrassed to stay, and conversation was difficult under the circumstances, which were that he wasn't going to get a chance to fish at all."

So Simon was put ashore, and waded out and started casting, with the inevitable result that, in no time, he was into another fish. That completed his quota of four, and once it was landed, he stayed on the beach while Michener had the boat to himself, actually hooking and landing a salmon just before lunch, greatly to Simon's relief, enabling him to resume normal conversation with the man who signed his warrant as deputy minister.

"It was," says Simon, "my longest morning, in spite of all the good luck."

His story reminded me of another of my favorite fishing companions, John Woods, of the great Ottawa family of outdoorsmen, and a man who looks so much like movie actor Jack Nicholson that he once caused a riot at a California resort merely by walking down to the pool. John cultivates the resemblance by rolling his eyes the way Nicholson does, sometimes all the way back into his head, leaving only the whites showing. In the rat race side of life, Woods directs the work of the Canadian Standards Council and travels widely, leading me to suspect that he is really our M, the head of the Canadian Secret Service, and that everything else, including his huntin' and fishin' activities, is a cover.

(Come to that, the same may be true for Reisman, but that is another book, for another author. If salmon fishing is a cloak for undercover work, it is damn clever of them to think of anything so pleasant, and at least it is something we are good at.)

Simon had not heard the John Woods story of an excess of good fishing, so I told him about it, as best I could remember John telling it to me over hours spent on the Old Fort.

John has a host of stories, one of my favorites having nothing to do with fishing, since it involves the Korean War and John's part as an officer in the Royal Canadian Regiment, an involvement that he continued in civilian life, to the point of always feeling at home in a white pith helmet, the dress headgear of the RCRs. The night *M*A*S*H* broadcast its last program, John came to a party at our house dressed in his full Korean combat rig, into which he was still able to fit, since he is that kind of guy.

His Korean story involved the arrival of the regiment at Pusan, the troops lining up on the dock, whereupon one of John's fellow officers, a fat fellow who shall remain nameless for he is still alive, fell into a grease pit on the dock and broke his leg. He was escorted to a hospital ship that was tied up nearby, and the regiment moved off to the combat zone and thought of him no more.

Three months later, John was on duty as staff officer at regimental headquarters when he observed a thin, bedraggled figure making his way up the hill. As he drew near, John recognized his compatriot who had fallen into the grease pit and was last seen headed for the hospital ship. John went to greet the new arrival and remarked on how he had lost weight.

"Lost weight!" sighed the officer "That's not all I've lost."

And then he unfolded his tale of woe.

The ship wasn't just any old hospital ship, it was Swedish.

It was filled with serious casualties from the fighting, and with Swedish nurses who were eager for able-bodied men.

Our Canadian wasn't exactly able-bodied, but his broken leg was the least of the injuries among the men on board, so as soon as they had him properly splinted and bandaged, those Swedish nurses went to work. After three months, our man was thin, and pooped, and ready to rejoin the regiment, whatever perils it might be facing in battle.

It was a case of too much of a good thing, which was the point of Simon's story, and also of John's adventure on the Matapedia River in the Gaspé.

John Woods's fishing for salmon started in 1961, six years after he left the army, and in five years fishing the best waters he caught only two grilse, on a single evening on the

Upsalquitch. He had two weeks fishing back to back on the Matapedia and the Kidgewick in 1965 without a single rise, and he came to be known as Jonah of the waters. Mind you, nobody was having all that much luck, for this was the low point of the salmon cycle and a time when the extinction of the species Salmo Salar was widely feared, leading to measures that have slowly built the stock back, until today, in some rivers, there are more salmon than anybody can remember.

On this 1966 trip, however, John Woods went to the Matapedia with his brother, Shirley, and General Roger Rowley, and the other two joked that having John along would not harm the fishing, since he never caught any, anyway.

The first morning on the river, John flogged the Angus Pool without avail, and after lunch decided to take action, in an effort to change his miserable luck. He went to Lapointe's Sporting Goods store in the village of Matapedia, and asked about a rod that had been in the store window since the year before. It being obvious that Monsieur Lapointe wanted the rod out of there, John bought it at a discount and left with the fine 8'4" Orvis cane rod under his arm. He rigged the rod for the evening fishing, and said it would be a different world. Brother Shirley and friend Roger urged him on, as good fishing companions should when anglers' luck is down.

That evening, just before sunset, it happened—John Woods's first salmon. He has fished seventeen rivers in the twenty-five years since, and says he'll never forget that one—twenty pounds of fish, landed in twenty-five minutes, on the Rusty Rat. That night, the fish was the subject of many toasts, because times were so lean.

Next morning, John's allotted pool was Jime's Rock, and on the third cast a fish took, lightly like a trout, though guide George Fitzgerald said it was more likely a small salmon. When the fish took its first jump it was like a time warp on the Matapedia, the kind John had heard his father and grandfather talk about, and grandfather had once landed a fifty-two-pounder on the Bonaventure. It took forty-five minutes to land this beauty, and it weighed in at thirty-six pounds, the largest taken on the Matapedia that year.

Companions Roger and Shirley were now not quite so supportive, and their faces betrayed the look known in angling circles as the long lip. Flushed with his success, John elected not to fish that afternoon and to leave the pools to his companions, who fished frantically, without avail.

Next morning, John and his rod returned to the Angus pool, and brought in a twenty-two-pounder.

At lunch, Shirley announced a fish had risen for him in Mirror Pool that morning, his only sign of action in the entire trip. Doubtless, he said, John would catch the fish that evening.

And that evening, John cast his Rusty Rat upon the waters and drew a big boil in the wake of the fly. A brief rest for a smoke, and then back, with the salmon striking so hard it almost wrenched the rod out of John's hand. It was the best fight of all, and the fish weighed twenty-six pounds.

The return to the Restigouche Hotel was tense, the score for the trip being four for John, and zilch for the experts, Shirley and Roger.

"Luck of the draw," said John suavely, looking and sounding more like Jack Nicholson than ever.

John thought so much of that cane rod he has had it refinished twice by the Orvis people, and he says it's still his favorite, though I've never known him to fish with anything but the latest in graphite, boron and whatever new materials materialize.

As for Shirley and Roger, they won't even talk about John's Big Trip.

And after hearing the story, Simon says he knows how they must have felt, because the Governor General reacted in much the same way that time on the Eagle, though he didn't say anything.

THE BONEFISH CHAMP

The phone rang, and it was John Woods himself, to say he had a story that had nothing to do with trout or salmon, but was a good one about bonefish, the fightingest fish, pound for pound, in the world. (I still can't bring myself to say gram for gram or kilo for kilo.)

I hustled over to the office he enjoys as Executive Director of the Standards Council of Canada, with its view across the Ottawa River to the Gatineau Hills, where John has his lakeside home. The office, like the house, has fishing mementos on every wall, and John himself is festooned with cufflinks and beltbuckles that are fishy, while remaining in the best of taste.

He greeted me with the Jack Nicholson eyeroll that is his speciality, and we got right down to it, because he had to catch a plane for China.

I had heard about bonefish from Ted Williams, during a get-together with him on New Brunswick's Campobello Island, but I had never gone after them myself, despite a holiday in an apartment building called Bonefish Tower, at Marathon on the Florida Keys. On that occasion, the only fishing was for grunts, aboard a gang boat called *The Marathon Lady*, when we learned that grunts really do grunt when caught—and a whole boat-load of people catching grunts can set up quite a racket. We found they taste great in boullaibaise.

Anyway, as John explained, bonefish are caught tradition-ally in the warm-water areas off the Florida Keys and in the Caribbean. He was invited by a group called the National Sporting Fraternity of the United States to take part in a bone-fishing tournament, using only the fly. As the only Canadian invited, John accepted and flew to the island of Exuma, where he found thirty Americans assembled, some of them noted fish-ing authors.

John had never fished bonefish before, and his guide showed him how to wade the flats at low tide, "Seemingly for-ever."

The fish are taken on the flats when the tide is coming in, and when it is going out, so one wades these flats barefoot, with water about halfway up the calf, and, as the guide ex-plained, you spot the bonefish ahead, keeping in mind their nickname of "the grey ghosts of the flats." They usually appear as a blur, and the idea is to cast a fly in front of them and start stripping it, and with luck, they will take.

"The only thing wrong with this," says John, "is that they are the spookiest fish I've ever seen. If the fly lands with a little plop, it will spook the whole school of fish. They just disappear. So you have to be very careful with your presentation."

For this tournament, there were three days of fishing, and for the first two days, Woods got advice every night on why he wasn't catching any fish, the Americans patronizing him more than he found comfortable.

The third day, he set out with a grand total of two bonefish, and two very tired feet that threatened to collapse under him. He drew a new guide called Clifford, described as one of the *bon vivants* of the island. He put John into his launch, and off they went across the open sea to a distant island. The tide was full high and was backed up into the mangroves, and John's heart sank, because there was no future in casting into the tangle of trees, the only place the fish might be at that time of day.

There he was, into his third day and no prospects for that morning, with the tide so high.

Clifford stopped the boat about fifty yards off the island, directly in front of a small, deep cove, and threw out the anchor. He sat there, staring at the island and saying nothing.

The boat was in about twenty feet of water, so John looked at him and said, "Clifford, what are we doing parked here?"

He said, "I think we gonna get some bonefish, mon."

"Bonefish? In twenty feet of water?"

"Yup, I'm just watchin'."

Ten minutes passed, and Clifford said, "We's gottem, sir. They's a big school of bonefish trapped in the cove."

"Trapped by what?"

"By that big barracuda over there, on the left."

Sure enough, swimming slowly back and forth to the left of the boat was the biggest barracuda John had ever seen in his life, holding there, waiting for the bonefish to come out.

"Throw the fly in there," said Clifford.

"Where?"

"Never mind where, just throw it."

So John pitched in, and, to make a long story short, by noon he had twenty-three bonefish in the boat, averaging five pounds. The tide went down, the fish departed with the barracuda in hot pursuit, and John picked up another two or three fish in the afternoon.

"You gonna be the winnah, mon, you sure gonna be the winnah!" Clifford shouted, jumping up and down, while John kept throwing the fly out with abandon after each fish was netted.

I asked how they fought, and John said the bonefish run much further than a salmon, but don't jump.

"When you hook them, they take off," he said, "and if you get into one, you better have two hundred yards of backing on the reel. That's a lot of backing for a five or six pound fish—my biggest was seven."

"But," I said, having read it somewhere, "they're no good to eat."

"They're wonderful," said John. "But difficult, because of the bones. The chef, my maid and the manager each looked for fish every day."

When he came in that night and announced his catch, in an offhand, informal way, as twenty-seven for the day, there was incredulity among the other competing anglers gathered at the Peace and Plenty Hotel.

They had to come out and verify it, and they did. That night was presentation night, and John Woods got the silver tray and all the freebies from the tackle manufacturers, for being bonefish champion. There was nobody even close—the real pros were getting five or six bonefish a day, so the trapped school just submerged the competition.

The president of the fraternity, Jim Rickoff, asked John privately how the hell he did it. John said he wasn't saying anything, and Clifford was sworn to silence about the secret cove.

"It shows you Lady Luck will sometimes be riding on your shoulder when things seem bleak."

"Lady Luck," I observed, "by the name of Clifford."

Yes, John agreed, adding that, since that occasion two years ago, he had been back to fish with Clifford and the performance was repeated, this time for a score of twelve.

The association has invited John Woods back for another bonefish tournament, but he prefers to retire undefeated, chalking one up for Canada (and Clifford).

THINKING SMALL

"Simon," I said, "do you really expect anybody to believe that, when the high rollers go fishing, they don't talk shop and make deals?"

He blinked.

"Did I say that?"

"You keep saying it every trip we talk about."

"Well, put it this way then," he chose his words even more carefully than usual, which is pretty careful. "People who fish together are more likely to deal together."

Pause.

"I mean," he expanded, "you get to know people and you get comfortable with them.

"Also," he laughed, "you get invited on more fishing trips."

But I pressed the matter of shop-talk, since, in my experience, the movers and shakers talk of little else, in action or in rare moments of repose. After all, Simon keeps describing himself as an intense fisherman, though he insists there are long periods of contemplation on the water.

I recalled to him a story told to me by novelist Roger Lemelin, who once served a term in the employ of Paul Desmarais, who made him publisher of *La Presse*, and hence eligible to fish as Desmarais's guest on Anticosti Island, in the fabled waters of the Jupiter.

A fellow guest in that party was John Robarts, the former premier of Ontario and, at the time, co-chairman of a Royal Commission on national unity, appointed by Pierre Trudeau.

Lemelin asked Robarts about his work, and was surprised to receive this reply: "I am in love, Roger!"

Roger, a romantic himself, was taken aback, and thought Robarts must be kidding. Or perhaps he found it hard to believe that any premier of Ontario could be in love.

"I am hopelessly besotted," said Robarts, a tear streaming down his face.

"Lucky fellow," said Lemelin, and proceeded to listen while Robarts poured out his soul.

"Well," said Simon, "that's a good story, but you wouldn't exactly call it shop talk."

"Okay then, sex talk. Is there much talk about sex?"

Simon said he couldn't remember any, adding he wouldn't tell me if he could. I had been on enough fishing trips to know, and I had to agree that the sex stories were few and far between, only getting personal when my companions tried to reason with me, when I was as smitten, as Robarts, by the second love of my life, and hopefully the last, because of the intensity of it. I told them all they should be so lucky, and usually that changed the subject.

Simon seemed uneasy with this turn in our talk, so he backtracked.

"When I'm with successful people," he said, "I usually ask them the secret of their success. And it brings some surprising answers."

"Like what?"

"Well, like the British lord whose answer was 'small things'."

Simon counts this nobleman among one of his most memorable fishing companions, and he talks about him almost with awe—not so much because of his nobility, but because of his ability with a rod.

Lord Verulum fished under the name of John Grimston, and he ran a variety of manufacturing concerns in Britain, which made him a customer of the Aluminum Company of Canada, and hence a guest on the Sainte-Marguerite.

Simon had never fished with a lord before, and was not sure what the protocol would be, especially when it was made known that His Lordship had his own salmon water in Scotland, and that fishing had run in the family at least as far back as the first Lord Verulum, Francis Bacon. Vast estates, lots of money and his own salmon water—the image was one of considerable magnificence, with rods galore and tweed wardrobes and servants dancing attendance.

When he arrived, Verulum fulfilled expectations in one respect—he called the guides "ghillies," in the Scottish fashion. But everything else about him was unconventional.

He brought with him two ancient greenheart rods, equipped with huge, old-fashioned reels, everything fastened together with tape. He brought no selection of flies, just a few Green Highlanders in different sizes. His fishing costume was a baggy a pair of grey flannels, brown oxford shoes with no socks, and a white shirt, and nothing else except a piece of rope used to hold up the trousers. For the cold weather, he had a tweed jacket full of holes, and a deerstalker hat that was the worse for wear. He not only fished in that outfit, he travelled in it as well, with a small duffel bag that contained an extra pair of trousers and another shirt. Verulum, it became clear, preferred to fish "wet," without any foul-weather gear—at day's end he hung one outfit up to dry and came to dinner in the back-up rig, keeping up this routine for an entire week of wet-weather fishing.

The old greenheart cane rods were about sixteen feet in length, and they were heavy, but Verulum was a tall man with muscles and he swung those rods by the hour, in the old two-handed way. Simon, a small man, tried to heft the rods and marvelled that anybody could handle them, let alone catch fish.

"Catch fish!" Simon marvels today. "Nobody on the river had ever seen anything like him. He knew how to read the river. He used those rods to such advantage that he could fish places nobody else could, because of the power of his casts. He would heave that line like you wouldn't believe. The guides developed so much respect for him that, on any day, none of them would want to fish a pool that Verulum had fished. They called him 'le grand pecheur'."

He developed cancer and, when told he was going to die, he went into seclusion and put his affairs in order, and on the Sainte-Marguerite they named a pool after him. It is still known as Verulum's Pool, because nobody but he ever took fish out of it."We couldn't reach it properly," says Simon.

One night during a poker game, Simon put his usual question to power anglers. "What is your secret? You're a successful businessman, you've made a lot of money, you've built up big businesses, to what do you attribute your success?"

Simon got what he calls a great answer.

"Simon," said Verulum, "I make little things, not big things. There are people who make ships, and aircraft, and cars, but not me. In the car business, I make fasteners, and washers, and they don't mind paying good prices for well-made little things. And the market is more diversified than for the big stuff, and steadier, too."

Simon's eyes light up when he repeats that story, just as they do when he recalls Verulum's pool and the sight of His Lordship taking an eighteen-pound salmon out of it.

All Simon ever got out of that pool was a sea trout, but he got a lot of mileage out of Verulum's success secret. He never did get invited to fish His Lordship's Scottish water, though Jake Warren did, when he was Canada's High Commissioner in London.

JAKE

Jake Warren figures in Simon's stories more than anybody else, so I went over to his highrise office in downtown Ottawa to check on the Lord Verulum and other tales, and I found him caressing—actually fondling—a gold-plated Sovereign salmon reel his wife had given him for his seventieth birthday.

It was the latest thing from the House of Hardy, by appointment to HRH the Prince of Wales, to mark a milestone in the history of the famous tackle makers and merchants, one-time rulers of the angling world when split bamboo was king. You dont see so many North American anglers using Hardy gear anymore, though most have some piece by Hardy in their kits. Jake admitted that most of his latter-day salmon fishing had been done with an Orvis rod and a Bodgon reel, given him by former Bank of Canada Governor Lou Rasminsky when he retired from the fishing frays.

As Canada's High Commissioner in the United Kingdom, Warren got to know a lot about Hardy's Fishing, as the firm's retail emporium on Pall Mall signs itself, and, though he was impressed by his gold-plated reel, he showed none of the awe for the old firm that colonials were wont to do earlier in the century. I recalled my father getting his first Hardy catalogue in 1931, and poring over its mysteries, most of them beyond the reach of New Brunswickers of the time, even though we assumed the famous St. John and St. George salmon reels were named for places in our province. Most New Brunswick anglers used hand-me-down equipment, and steel telescopic rods were much in fashion, with Hardy's Palakona the stuff of dreams. As for the spinning reels making their first appearance in the catalogue, Canadian fishermen would have to wait through the Depression and the War before finding out about those, when nylon monofilament replaced catgut, a breakthrough as profound as the replacement of wooden boat hulls by fibreglass, or canned orange juice by frozen, or wrinkled shirts by wash and wear.

I didn't want to diminish Jake's joy at his gold-plated Hardy reel, but I told him about my own all-time fishing companion, Jack Sanderson, and his run-in with Hardy's before the War. Sandy bore no grudge against the firm and, in fact, got me going on buying their stuff, much of which I still have in reserve for the day when we all go back to bamboo rods and leather wallets for flies, and leather-trimmed rod cases that reek of the Raj.

As Canadian Press correspondent in London in the '30s, Sanderson covered the abdication and the Munich appeasement and the outbreak of war, drawing on his friend Mike Pearson, who fed him tips from Canada House, in return for which Sanderson advised Pearson on what a Canadian diplomat should wear to the coronation of King George VI. (There being no prescribed protocol, they made one up, gold braid, leggings and all.)

CP did not pay well, and Sandy was hard-pressed to keep his end up in London, though he was helped by the fact that he was a tall man of aristocratic mien, and would have made a marvellous duke in the eighteenth century, or maybe even the nineteenth. Through his early years in Canada, he had built up a knowledge of fishing that was awesome, and it was one of his life's ambitions to own a Hardy rod.

When he came into a small windfall, he decided the time had come, so he ventured into the Pall Mall sanctorum, full of anticipation mixed with awe. He knew in advance the attendants wore frock coats and striped trousers, and he had heard it was well to have an introduction to the firm before attempting to do business. In those days, five-pound notes were printed on light linen paper of folio size, and ten-pound notes were even bigger, requiring folding to fit in a pocket, and needing to be signed when cashed. Sandy had seen neither the five nor the ten before, but when he went to Hardy's that day, he had one of each on his person, and thus was emboldened to face whate'er betide.

A lordly gentlemen in a clawhammer coat eventually recognized his presence, after several minutes of being ignored. Sandy was inspecting a rack of trout rods when he was challenged to state his business, and he said he would like to buy one of the rods, a light one of the kind in the rack marked *trout*.

To the question of what country, and what fish, Sandy replied that he would be using it in Canada, on large-mouth bass.

"Not one of our trout rods, sir," came the reply. "They are not for coarse fishing, you understand."

Sandy gathered that, somewhere in the bowels of the shop, there were rods for coarse fishing, though the kind of sportsmen who patronized Hardy's would not be likely to go in quest of them.

"I understand no such thing," he snorted. "Do your rods here have prices on them?"

"We keep our price list separate," he was told.

"Could I see it?"

"Why, yes."

A pause, while the list was produced.

"Do I not have money here in my hand?" said Sandy, waving his five and ten-pound notes.

"Yes, sir, you do."

"And is it any of your goddamned business what I do with the rod when I have bought it?"

"I suppose not, sir."

"You suppose correctly. Can I not use the rod to prop up a clothesline if I want to?"

"Certainly, sir, if you are so disposed. Yes, sir, you could, but we would not advise it."

Sandy handed over the banknotes and took the rod away with him, in its fancy blue cloth cover, and he brought it back to Canada and fished with it for years, sometimes for trout, but more often for bass, which he insisted gave a better fight on the fly than either speckled trout or rainbows. He bought a lot more Hardy gear before the onset of fibreglass, graphite, boron and other man-made blanks pushed bamboo into the dark ages of angling, and for a while he became convinced the spinning rod would put fly fishing out of business, even succumbing to a new plastic device that was claimed to make it possible to cast a fly with a spinner. None of this bothered him, since he counted every day spent fishing as a day gained, regardless of what he had in his hand.

I was with him on his happiest day, below an old milldam in Northern Québec, when he threw a dry fly over some foaming water and a two-pound speckled trout rose and took it in mid-air. He said he had waited all his life for that moment.

During the recounting of this tale, Jake Warren kept admiring his gold-plated reel and savoring the memory of the birthday party in London at which he had received it, in the presence of a throng of British friends and admirers.

Reisman had said to get Warren's follow-up on the Lord Verulum story, since Warren had been a guest on Verulum's own waters on the River Ness. Warren laughed, and said the experience very nearly got him in the Guiness Book of Records for the fastest trans-Atlantic salmon catch on record.

On the eve of taking up his post as Canadian High Commissioner in London, Warren took a farewell fling at Labrador's Eagle River, courtesy the Canadian Armed Forces, and he came away pleased with himself, having been top rod for the week, outfishing his fellow public servants, who were there together with a clutch of American generals who had fished very hard.

"I came off the river very full of myself," he says, "forgetting that fishing is supposed to be a lesson in humility."

Warren flew from Labrador to Montréal and boarded the plane there for London, carrying his prize salmon with him. At Gatwick Airport he was met by the High Commission limousine, which whisked his salmon to the Mayfair residence, while Warren went directly north to Inverness, where Lord Verulum had invited him to fish his salmon waters.

"John met me with two rods under his arm," says Warren, "and he had us on the water faster than you could say *jetlag*. I only had that afternoon, because I had to be back in London the following day."

Midway through the afternoon, Warren hooked a big salmon, and lost it.

Toward day's end, he got into another one, and he lost that, too.

"I lost them right under the noble lord's nose," he recalls, "and for reasons that evidently were not the fault of the fish."

What ran through his mind was the old saying, *Never pretend to understand Japanese culture, and never be proud of your skills as a salmon fisherman*. He had been fishing the Eagle in Labrador only the day before, so it would have been a unique double if he had been able to pull it off. As luck would have it, the power failed at the High Commission in London, the freezer thawed, and all the Labrador fish were lost.

Was Verulum critical?

"Not at all," says Warren. "But he taught me something. He seemed to like Simon and me from our encounters on the Sainte-Marguerite. He found us strange and odd, but he was warm toward both of us.

"He knew I was new to the job of High Commissioner, so he drew me aside as I was leaving and presented me with a salmon that someone else had taken, and he put it in a sleeve— a sort of wicker envelope with a handle on it. Thats the way they present fish to guests who are on their way home.

"As he gave it to me, *en route* to the railway station, he said there were only two things I needed to know to be successful with the British. One was that when I was invited to a country house, I should always pay for my long-distance telephone calls. Guests, especially from North America, were notoriously careless about this and some hosts had installed pay phones in the bedrooms as a result.

"The other thing was that whenever I was given a salmon in one of those wicker sleeves, always remember the sleeve has to be returned. If I could remember those two things, I would have no trouble with the British."

Did I know that the original Roman capital of Britain was Verulinium, and that Verulum's title goes back to Sir Francis Bacon?

"And the Roman ruins of Verulinium are visible there at St. Albans, in Hertfordshire."

Warren did not return to Verulum's waters, "but you may be sure I sent back that wicker sleeve!"

"Tell me," I asked Jake Warren, "about the time you senior public servants got together to save Pierre Trudeau's bacon, by defeating the Government of Canada."

"Whoa, there," said Jake, wrinkling that forehead the way he does, and squinting those eyes. "Where did you ever get that idea?"

I said bits and pieces of it had been floating around, but nobody had ever been able to put together the story of how somebody in the Department of Public Works had the bright idea of turfing the prime minster out of the Harrington Lake estate that is reserved for his use, and finding him another rural hideaway that would give him more seclusion, thus opening Harrington and its five thousand acres of parkland to the public. Pierre Trudeau had let it be known through official channels that the only attractive thing about official life in Ottawa was the lake and all that went with it, and that if they wanted him out of there, they would have to blow him out.

Things were moving toward a showdown, when the members of the White Pine Fishing Club became aware that somebody, they were not sure who, was trying to buy the property from its owners, the Boy Scouts of Canada. The senior public servants who made up the White Pine membership had been leasing Fauquier Lake for years, with an option to buy, enjoying even better trout fishing than their mandarin neighbors at the more famous Five Lakes Fishing Club.

The Boy Scouts asked for bids, and let it be known that they had one of $72,000, so the senior civil servants begged and borrowed as much as they could to scrape together the amount, and with the help of a couple of anonymous "angels," they sent in their matching bid, saying they wanted to exercise their option.

The reply from the Scouts was that it was puzzling to have two identical bids from the Government of Canada.

This was puzzling, because the mandarins were bidding as private citizens, and said so.

"We thought you guys *were* the government," said the Scouts.

"Nobody here but us ordinary people," came the reply, perhaps the first time senior public servants ever referred to themselves in such modest terms. Then, after a pause, "Who entered the other bid?"

"Sorry, we'd better not say," said the Scouts, taking cover.

The public servants compared notes and remembered they had wondered about some familiar figures they had seen poking around the fishing premises—people they knew were associated with the Department of Public Works and the Privy Council Office, none of them of the angling kind. They put two and two together, and upped their bid, with the help of some mortgage loans, exercised their option and got the place, where they have continued to fish happily ever since.

As for Trudeau, he stayed on at Harrington Lake, and liked it so much he held on even after he quit the prime ministership and left politics. He would not yield the estate to his successor, John Turner, until finally he was evicted, and Brian Mulroney took over what is the largest outdoor spread available to any elected head of government, anywhere in the world.

It was at Harrington Lake that a younger John Turner had courted Princess Margaret in their salad days, and it was there that Pierre Trudeau romanced both Barbra Streisand and Margaret Sinclair, who described herself as "Pierre's country mistress," before they were wed and she turned the garden into an organic health-food farm, to the despair of the park wardens who had to look after the crop, while worrying about Pierre and Maggie tramping through the wilderness unguarded.

As for the fishing at Harrington Lake, there are conflicting reports, though poachers from nearby Québec hamlets say they have no complaints. John Diefenbaker used to say the fishing was great, and he took Dwight Eisenhower out for a couple of cracks at it. Lester Pearson used to say it was "okay," and so far as is known, Pierre Trudeau never fished it at all, telling one press conference that the idea of a hook in a fish's mouth repelled him. Brian Mulroney says the fishing is "just so-so," and that the kids enjoy water skiing more. (With Trudeau, it was high diving.)

The adjoining lake to the south is Lake Meech, famed as the place of no Accord, but quite well regarded in fishing circles for its grey trout. And the northern neighbor of Harrington is Lac Philippe, which used to have the reputation of the best fly fishing for smallmouth bass in Western Québec. It is now the locale of the biggest public campground in the National Capital Area, and the fishing has gone to pot.

In one of our early talks, Jake Warren had given me his appraisal of Simon Reisman as a fishing companion, and what he said was that Reisman was a purposeful angler, passionate, dedicated, determined energetic, competitive, first out in the morning, last in at night. I think he may also have used the word *fierce*. Most of the adjectives were ones I had heard Simon apply to himself, so there were no surprises—Simon's wife had said, after all, that she imagined he went about fishing much the way he went about life.

And then the phone rang, and it was Jake, wanting to add something to his appraisal of Simon on the water. "I forgot to say," he said, "that he is also a very *good* fisherman." I said I had taken that for granted, but Warren wanted to elaborate, saying Simon was not only good at hooking and landing fish, he was good at reading water and knowing where to cast, when to move and when to stay, when to change flies and what flies to change to.

"You sound like you're in a talkative mood," I said, having known times when Jake was not. "Mind if I come over?"

Jake said to come ahead, and soon I was seated in one of the offices of the Québec Bureau in Ottawa, that equivalent of an embassy where Warren, having served the Canadian government most his life, now works as an adviser and trade negotiator for the Government of Québec, in which capacity he keeps an eye on some of the world's best trout and salmon fishing when he's not representing Québec at international confabs.

I opened with the hardest question for an angler to answer— "Tell us about your most memorable fish."

Jake rose to it "The largest fish I have killed," he said, in that soft voice of his, "was twenty-nine-and-a-half pounds, and it was taken out of a pool in the Sainte-Marguerite which was not operating properly. In connection with the construction of a road from Chicoutimi to Tadoussac, they had come quite close to the bank of the river and had built a little barrier over which the fish were supposed to go, but the fish were congregating in the pool below and not going up.

"They weren't in normal lies, and the water was kind of swirling below the barrier. I threw my fly in and suddenly a great gallumph took place, and off we went and running. One could tell by the play that it was a large fish. After about twelve or fourteen minutes the action stopped. We were on the east side of the river, away from the highway, and people were standing. Suddenly I heard my guide, who was standing beside me, shouting to the spectators: *"Lance une rouche!"* He repeated the cry several times, until one of the men got the message and tossed a huge boulder into the pool. The fish went off like a rocket, and five minutes later we had him on the beach. I enjoyed that enormously."

And the longest fight?

That would also be on the Sainte-Marguerite.

"David Culver, who subsequently became head of Alcan, was fishing the pool above me, about three miles up the river we were. Suddenly, out of the white water above my pool, came a canoe, with the guide and Culver with his wide fedora hat, and a fish on. They went through our pool and down into more white water, spilt, got up and got the canoe organized, and went on down past the camp, and into a mile-and-a-half of water before the Sainte-Marguerite joins the Saguenay. The fish was still on and fighting, until they got almost to the junction of the two rivers, when the fish came to the net.

"As the guide lifted the net under him, the fish spit out the fly, and the fish went out into the water and away. Now remember, that fight covered more than three miles of river and lasted four hours before the fish, at the very last moment, escaped. David was disappointed, but all of us felt the greatest respect for this wonderful, wonderful fish and its great battle."

There were times, I agreed, when the direct approach is best, and delicacy be damned.

Which brought Jake to a story of something that happened on the Eagle, when he was fishing with the U.S. Chief of the Defence Staff, Admiral Tom Mourer.

The party gathered for a drink in the lounge tent, before going to the mess tent for dinner after a day of fishing, and Admiral Mourer asked if anybody knew the fastest time for landing a salmon. Everybody described their fastest fish, and when the stories had gone the rounds, Mourer breathed a sigh and said, "I guess I'm the fastest rod in the East."

He had been fishing that day in the Bathtub Pool, below the falls, a place where the water rushes and seethes, not the usual placid pool, but a place where fish were known to congregate and take.

As the Admiral told it, he cast into the foam and there was an immediate tug and the whir of the reel, as the fish headed down with the current. Suddenly it turned, the line went slack, the fish streaked back upstream and jumped, landing in the boat, where, as the Admiral said, he wrestled it to the ground.

I asked if all of Jake's stories were about Atlantic salmon, and he said no, harking back to a holiday in southern France, near the Dordogne, where, as a visiting ambassador, Warren had introductions to the local gentry, including one elegant lady who wrote letters and invitations on parchment, which she rolled into scrolls, sealed with wax and mailed. She found that Warren was interested in fishing, and courteously offered to fix him up.

Early in the morning, Warren went to her house, where he was picked up by a gentleman who drove him away without exchanging a word. After an hour's drive, they turned down a lane and came to a pond that was mostly covered with green algae. The guide produced a light line out of his pocket, the smallest hook Warren had ever seen, and a handful of barley grains that had been soaked overnight in water. A tiny bobbin was attached, the barley was put on the hook, and, in Warrens words, "we went fishing."

The two men sat there for several hours, and every so often the bobbin would twitch, and a fish would be landed, the average length being between two and three inches.

"We got five or six of them during the day," recalls Jake. "I wrote a letter to that lady to tell her I had never had such fishing, which was no more than the truth."

And yet, I remarked, the day had struck in Warren's mind, as memorable as any he had spent on great rivers, after great fish, which just went to show there was no bad fishing, just as there is no bad wine, and no bad whisky, only degrees of goodness.

Having celebrated his seventieth birthday, what were Jake Warren's plans for this summer's fishing?

He reeled it off: June to Stewart Island on the West Coast, as a member of the board of the company that makes Peterbilt and Kenworth trucks; mid-July to the Sand Hill in Labrador; August to the Sainte-Marguerite. Meantime, a little trout fishing at the White Pine. "Can't complain," said Warren, with a twinkle.

Jake Warren married an Irish girl, whom he met when she was on holiday in Canada, and the marriage led him to some good fishing in Ireland.

"My father-in-law," he recalls fondly, "at my suggestion, had organized my honeymoon, which would take place at various fishing hotels. His name was Jack Titterington, and he was captain of that great golf club Royal County Down, and a great sport.

"Anyway, it had been so arranged, and we had many delights, fishing, as well as all the warmth and wonderfulness of a honeymoon. Out at Waterville, which is a hotel that sits almost on a beach, with a short run of water out of a long lake that parallels the shore. It has salmon and sea trout, and in the hallway of the hotel is a big marble block where occasionally a trophy fish is displayed.

"They put me in the hands of a nice ghillie, and I trotted out the spinning rod and fly rod I'd brought from Canada, and he watched me do my stuff. Remember, this was before I'd been to the Sainte-Marguerite or ever seen an Atlantic salmon. So he said to me, 'Mr. Warren, why don't you go up to the weir, and you'll have some fun with the trout. I'll just fish here awhile for the salmon.' So he went to work with a big rod, and in no time there was a big commotion and he was into a fish, which headed for the sea, splashing right across the sand in the shallow water. He brought it in and it was big, all right. Biggest fish I'd ever seen.

"It was his fish, as far as I was concerned. We went back to the hotel and Joan and I went hand in hand for a nice walk and, when we came back, all the old retired brigadiers and such were standing around the block of marble, so I eased my way over to see what the action was, and there, by gum, was the big fish. They had been told it was the young Canadian's, so they all started to congratulate me. I said there was a misunderstanding, since I had not caught the fish at all, the ghillie had. But they all insisted 'Your fish, old man. Your fish.' It turned out the fish was not a salmon, but a sea trout, the first one of the year and the largest that had been taken in four years. That's when I began to learn about Old Country fishing."

F ish stories should lose nothing in the telling, and so it is
with some of my favorites, recounted herewith in their latest versions, by way of topping off our
tales. Like all that has gone before,
they are more about people than
about fish—or rather, they are about
what happens to people when they
fish, usually bringing out the best in
them, but not always. The stories
come out fun side up.

MORLEY

Morley Safer was not a fishing companion, because he did not fish and, in fact, said he hated fishing. But the aid he rendered to four striken anglers on the ponds of Newfoundland's Avalon Peninsula will never be forgotten by those he saved, and is a part of early television lore, as an example of the early comradeship of the trade.

It happened during the 1957 Canadian election, when we were breaking new ground by covering the election campaign in the field, with the first crew ever sent out from CBC News headquarters in Toronto. Everything we did was a "first," from filming pieces in the dome car of CPR's Canadian, to the erection of a commemorative cairn in the ravine of the North Saskatchewan River at Edmonton. And everywhere we went, we were oddities in what was still the realm of print journalism, but the stuff we sent back got on the air at a time when the CBC had a TV monopoly in Canada. There was a stirring of interest across the land, which may have been of some help to the eventual upset winner, John Diefenbaker, who came across on TV as a sort of avenging evangelist, seeking to save the nation from the Liberal sinners. (When he won, Diefenbaker took a few days fishing before coming to Ottawa, to collect his prize and start a feud with CBC TV that dogged him throughout his time as prime minister, and contributed to his eventual defeat.)

Our small band of pioneers little thought that the cumbersome tools we were carrying would eventually come to dominate Canadian elections, to the point where they would become primarily photo opportunities, and that television would be the major factor in deciding, not only who wins elections, but who gets chosen to campaign in them.

I was the on-camera correspondent in the team, and the crew chief was Morley Safer, which meant he saw there was film for the camera and that the stuff we shot got shipped back to Toronto by the first available TCA plane (like the Canadian Broadcasting Corporation, Trans-Canada Airlines, later Air Canada, had a monopoly, too.)

Our travels took us to St. John's, Newfoundland, where we shot such spectacles as the departure of the "trouters' special," the train that left the city in early morning and dropped anglers off at selected spots along the track to a distance of a hundred miles, picking them up on the return journey. We were cautioned not to try to film the arrival of the train back in town, because it was not a pretty spectacle, and even on departure there was a heavy odor of Screech through the cars, Screech being the dregs of the rum barrels. It was so named by American troops stationed in Newfoundland during the war, because that's what it made them do when they drank it.

Heavy fog descended, engulfing everything in sight or, more properly, hiding it. We couldn't shoot, and couldn't have shipped anything if we did. Thus imprisoned, we had no choice but to relax and enjoy, and in those days, there was little to do in Newfoundland but fish.

The local CBC people, mostly veterans of the Newfoundland Broadcasting Corporation, which came as part of the package when the island voted so narrowly to join Canada in 1949, were hospitable, and suggested we do a little trouting, promising that there were virgin ponds within reach, never fished by man or beast. The weather was cold—the pack ice was still on the ocean off St. John's Harbor, and the harbor entrance was partially blocked by a huge iceberg. We had no fishing clothes and no tackle, but our hosts promised to equip us, so we agreed to an early morning start, provided the fog hadn't lifted, so we could escape back to Mainland Canada.

Morley Safer opted out of our excursion, saying he would rather stay in town and watch the fog, which turned out to be the first of many good decisions he made during his subsequent distinguished career.

We had equipped ourselves with an outsized bottle of overproof rum against the chill, Newfoundland being one of the two places you could get overproof, the other being the Yukon, where it was permitted because it wouldn't freeze, and kept consumers from doing so.

The Avalon Peninsula abounds in ponds, some of which are lakes and some are puddles, and we threaded our way through the rocky landscape until we reached the appointed spot and got out of the car.

To describe the scene as bleak would be understating it—rocks, fog, cold wind whipping waves on the water, and nothing to encourage anticipation in the angler except the idea of a swig of that rum. We all took a mouthful, savoring the thought of the sun-drenched island where the sugar grows, and then we split up, each of us going to our designated pond, and agreeing to meet every hour for a restorative sip.

I waded into my pond, and all thought of virgin waters vanished when I found myself up to my ankles in old sardine cans, ketchup bottles, and empties of liquor and beer. Anglers had indeed been here before, and at least that led to the thought that there must be trout. Alas, there was no sign, and my casts became the half-hearted kind when the angler feels it is all in vain. I kept casting to keep my circulation going while awaiting the first rum rendezvous.

Less than half an hour had passed when the expedition leader and host, Newfoundland broadcaster Ted Brophy, came looming out of the fog in my direction, stumbling over the rocks and uttering sounds that I took to be Newfoundland curses—I couldn't be sure, because among the things they do differently in Newfoundland is use cuss words unknown to the outside world, though their tone conveys the meaning. I was glad to see Brophy, because he had taken the bottle of rum with him and his early arrival raised the promise that I might not perish from the cold. But as he drew near, I could see that he was walking strangely, and that his clothes were a darker hue than they had been when he set out, the reason being that he was dripping wet, from his silver hair to the bottoms of his hip waders.

I inquired after his health, while fearing for my own.

"Fell in!" he gasped.

"You must be cold!"

"That I am, but that's not the worst of it, me son."

(Newfoundlanders call everybody "me son," even women, though they do recognize the difference, to judge by the birth rate.)

When Brophy came alongside he opened the top of his wicker creel, in which he had placed the sacred bottle only thirty minutes before. There was nothing there but a pitiful pile of broken glass, the biggest piece with the label attached, and the neck with the cap still screwed on tight.

"You lost it all?" I whimpered.

He nodded. "All but the smell, and whatever went down into my rubber boots."

My spirits quickened at the thought of the boots having some rum in them, though they looked the worse for wear. "How old are those boots?" I inquired.

"Not sure," said the shivering Brophy. "I got them from my dear dead father thirty years ago, and I never knew how long he might have had them before that."

Prospects were not bright, but I invited him to sit down on a rock while I pulled the hip waders off him. In the boundless realm of fishing and drinking lore, what followed was a horror story.

When the first boot came free there was lots of liquid sloshing around in its dark innards, and I stuck my nose down the top, took a deep sniff, and reeled back in shock. In my native New Brunswick, it had long been the custom to buy empty rum barrels from the liquor commission and build a fire under them, putting some water inside and swishing it around, and when steam was generated, you put your head in the barrel and inhaled the fumes, as a result of which you got swished. But this was another and darker world inside those boots of Brophy. The effluvium that emerged from the dark recesses of the first boot comprised, I subsequently concluded, the smells of feet, old socks, old rubber, decayed canvas, decades of fish scales, musty cupboards and car trunks. Only faintly discernible in the background was the smell of overproof rum.

I dumped some of the liquid onto the rocks, reflecting that, in color and texture, it resembled the crankcase oil of a vehicle that has never had a change. We ruled it to be undrinkable, despite the desperation of our circumstances. The contents of the second boot were of no better quality than the first, so all we could do was sniff, and try to isolate the aroma of the rum from the rest. It was small comfort.

The others joined us, and there was no need to inquire after the fishing luck, because there was none. We built a fire to dry Brophy out—there were some twigs around, but where they came from I don't know, because there were no trees. We commiserated with one another and talked about our next move, each of us wondering if it would be polite to suggest a withdrawal to the distant city.

Just then, through the distant fog, we perceived the figure of a man, headed in our direction. When he drew near, lo, it was Morley. How had he found us? What was he doing here? Had the fog lifted at the airport so we could fly out? None of these questions came to mind. What came to mind was whether he had any rum on him.

"Did you bring any?" I called out.

"Any what?" came the reply.

"Rum."

"You brought some, didn't you?"

(Even then, Safer was a good interviewer.)

"All gone."

"You drank it already?"

"No. Broke it."

"God, it's cold," said Morley. "I got bored in town and found a cab driver who knew where you'd be, because this is where they bring visitors from away."

"Morley," I interrupted. "Got anything to drink on you?"

"Oh, sure," he said. "You wouldn't think I'd come out here with nothing?" He reached into the pocket of his jacket and produced a mickey of rum.

We contemplated it, each of us thinking about the lost forty-ouncer.

The mickey would have to do for the four of us, excluding the donor, who, after all, had not been through what we anglers had. We grabbed the bottle, and each of the four fishermen took great swigs, and it was gone. With that, the sun came out, and the day was saved, and we fished on without result, and Morley returned to St. John's, confirmed in his belief that all fishermen had to be crazy.

I have carried a warm spot in my heart for Morley Safer ever since, and have forgiven him everything in his glamorous television career, though I've noticed he has never done much election coverage, and so far as I know, has never fished.

As for me, I came away from our adventure convinced that, if there are trout in Newfoundland, they are there for the natives and not the visitors, just as in Nova Scotia. Any reference to the contrary in the tourist literature is a fraud.

GIL

I had not intended to write about Gil Purcell because, as has been said in other volumes, he tends to dominate any book he gets into. One story might keep him in his place, along with a note about who he was, and what.

What he was, was the conscience of the news business for the better part of forty years, and if you think the news business has no conscience, you didn't know Purcell. As poohbah of the agency known as Canadian Press, he instilled fear in his staff, along with a measure of respect and, in notable cases, affection. He was a martinet about style, spelling and facts, and he had the eye of an eagle, combined with the memory of an elephant. He had one leg, and he drank rum, and he fished so assiduously he dominated every tournament he entered, including the Interprovincial Bass Derby, over which he ruled, representing his native Manitoba and setting contest rules so complex that only he and his most ardent disciples understood them.

His passion for detail extended to his scanning of the Canadian Press news file, and in particular he insisted that, whenever an amputee was mentioned, it be made clear whether the leg had come off above the knee, or below. His was above, so he knew how profound the difference is. His favorite fishing companion was author and editor Ralph Allen, and it was Purcell's habit to invite other war amps to accompany them, which meant Allen always had to carry the outboard motor and the other gear, leading him to lament that Purcell was big on people who had no arms or no legs and "one day he'll invite somebody who has no head!"

Purcell walked with a stick when he had his artificial leg on, and when he didn't, he used crutches, especially on fishing trips. On one trip in Northern Québec, we had to cross a bog to get to the boat, and when Purcell reached forward with his crutches they went straight down into the ooze, leaving him prostrate with his face stuck in the mud.

My fondness for Purcell was deepened when he looked up at me, blinked his eyes to get the goo out of them, and laughed. Anybody in his predicament who could do that couldn't be all bad, but there were other times when you wondered.

This story is about one of those times.

I had returned from a pilgrimage to the Normandy beaches, in the course of which I had written about how Charles de Gaulle, as president of France, was being beastly to the Canadians and wouldn't let any member of the Canadian cabinet attend the ceremonies at the Canadian war cemeteries there. The story caused a commotion and brought denials from the Canadian government, anxious to preserve the illusion of good relations with France.

Upon my return, I joined Purcell & Co. at a paper company trout camp north of Montréal. At the first breakfast he braced me about the Normandy hoo-hah, and expressed the opinion that I had blown it and got the facts wrong. I came back with the view that it was sour grapes on his part, because Canadian Press had missed the story, but he wasn't having any of that and kept giving it to me good, until I rose in heat and stormed out of the dining hall, straight down to the shore, where my guide was waiting with the gear in the canoe.

"Take me," I growled, "as far from Purcell as you possibly can, with all speed!"

The guide had never heard of Purcell, but he got the message and off we went, heading up the chain of lakes and along the posh portages with their wall-to-wall carpeting of pine needles, not pausing to fish until we had four lakes between us and my tormentor.

Eventually I cooled down and started to fish, but my concentration was off. Either that, or the paper company had neglected to stock the lakes that week, there being no publishers in attendance. I resigned myself to the blessed silence and the scenery, and the day passed peacefully, helped by an ample lunch and my flask of sugar cane brandy, until I remembered that this was Purcell's favorite tipple, too.

By the time we reached the outermost lake on the paper company limits it was getting to quitting time, when a truck would pick us up with our canoe and take us back to camp, as was the custom. The guide, accustomed to the ways of publishers when they have come for good fishing and get nothing, asked if I would really like to catch a trout, promising me "a canteloupe."

"Cantaloupe?" I said in surprise. "You have a cantaloupe?"

He pointed to the lake water.

"*Cantaloupe!*" he said. "*Beaucoup cantaloupe?*"

He wiggled his hand in fishy fashion, and indicated a fish of some significance by stretching out his arms.

"*Cantaloupe!*"

I tried to leap across the language barrier.

"Trout?"

"*Oui, de Colombie Britannique.*"

The light came on.

"Kamloops!" I said. "They put in Kamloops trout?"

"*Oui, monsieur,*" said the guide. "*Cantaloupe!*"

From the gunwale of the canoe he brought out his secret weapon, the willow tree of spinners and flashers and reflectors

and noisemakers supposedly forbidden in the realm of fly fishing, though familiar to guides in all parts of the country, and I
suspect all parts of the world, when the fly fails to produce.

He tied this vast apparatus onto my line and instructed me
to troll while he paddled around the lake. My poor little fly rod
bent under the strain and my fishing arm began to ache, when
all of a sudden there came an enormous tug on the line—not
the tickle of a trout but the pull of a monster fish, which sur-
faced with a swirl, showing a dorsal fin like that of a shark, before plunging to the bottom and sulking there.

I was nursing the fish when there were sounds from the
shore, and the truck pulled up at the landing and out stepped
Purcell, who had come along for the ride, having had a successful day's angling close to the camp.

My sorrow at seeing him was heightened by the realization
that he had caught me in the act, and my premonition of disaster was confirmed immediately when the fish started to stir.

Purcell saw my rod bent under the strain and he shouted
encouragement. "Oh, good man! Bloody fine show, old boy!"
He clapped his hands and the guide joined in, happy that he
had got his sport into a fish.

Just then, the monster fish broke water right in front of
where Purcell was standing, as he was asking what fly I had
got him on. The entire length of the fish was revealed, along
with that terrible train of hardware. There was a clatter when
all that spinning metal re-entered the water, and the din was
still echoing when, his face contorted with contempt, Purcell
shouted, "Son of a bitch! Bastard!"

Like the lover caught with another man's wife, there was
nothing to be said, but I mumbled something about it having
been a long day on the water, and that the guide made me do it
because he wanted to show me a Kamloops trout in Québec,
but nothing would check the torrent of criticism form the shore.

Mercifully, the trout shook himself off before he could be
netted, thus removing the evidence of my crime, and enabling
me to enter vehement denials when we got back to camp and
Purcell told his side of the story.

Through all the years after that, and on many fishing expeditions, he never let me forget it, nor did he cease dwelling on
my other sins and shortcomings, and those of others, especially
people in his employ. But we fished with him, and I gave him

my fishing hat made by Lock & Co., hatters for Hardy Bros., and when we buried Purcell the family gave me the hat back. It is on my head as I write, a size 7 ¾, the largest made—Purcell and I had two of the biggest heads in the business. But I had the advantage of him in one department. Two legs really are better than one, especially on the trails.

FRANK

Frank Swanson was a big, raw-boned redhead from Edmonton whose claims to fame included the fact that his engineer father designed the High Level Bridge across the North Saskatchewan River, and that when he played for the Edmonton Eskimos in the '30s, his pay was a ten-dollar bill left in his boot, and the day he led his tank regiment across the Sangro River in Italy. The crossing of the Sangro wasn't as heroic as it might sound, because the regimental commander had left the unit for the day and Captain Swanson's job was to look after things. Suddenly, the order came through to cross the Sangro, so Swanson rallied the troops and across they started. When the C.O. returned and saw the commotion, he roared, "What the hell do you think you are doing, Swanson?"

"Crossing the Sangro, sir," came the reply, and cross it they did. You can find it in the history books, it was a famous victory.

Swanson, or Svensen as I always called him, because he could act Swedish when he wanted to, was also a fisherman of note, and he introduced me to trout fishing, Old Ottawa Family Style, through the oldest fishing club in Western Québec, the Denholm Angling Club on Lac Saint-Germain, back of Poltimore in the Gatineau Hills.

The Denholm was so old nobody could remember when it started, except that early Governors General had belonged to it, and one of the best fishing spots was named Minto after the GG of that name. In those times the way Ottawa anglers got to the Denholm was by steamer down the Ottawa to Masson, by coach up the hill to Buckingham, by steamer up the Lievre to Notre Dame de la Salette, and they by buckboard cross-country to Poltimore, and up a steep wagon trail to the lake. It was a long day's journey and, once there, the party would stay for at least two weeks, enjoying fabulous fly fishing for speckled trout and a species known as Marstoni, which seemed to be indigenous to Lac Saint-Germain.

The trout were so plentiful there was a legend that, in earliest times, the lake was netted commercially to provide fish for the market in Bytown, which is what Ottawa was called before it became the capital.

By the time I joined the Denholm, at Swanson's invitation, the fly fishing was just about finished and the anglers were using spinners and, in some cases, worms. I have mentioned this in an earlier chapter, but bear with me, because I still dream about what the fly fishing must have been like when old Minto had the run of it, and the anglers wore bowler hats and high celluloid collars.

Swanson was one of those before-breakfast fishermen, believing that being on the water before dawn enabled one to surprise the fish before they were fully awake. It was through this technique that he caught the biggest Marstoni ever seen in the club, a fish of two-and-a-half pounds, so unusual it was sent off to the fish and game people in Québec City for analysis and entry in the record books. They sent it back with a note that, translated, meant "damned if we know," and the fish never did get the recognition it deserved.

Swanson was a good fishing companion, talkative when he was happy and silent when surly, which was often—he rose to be editor of *The Ottawa Citizen*, a job that would try the temper of the most serene, which Frank was not. He was rescued from insanity by an appointment as publisher of *The Calgary Herald*, ushering in a stormy but prosperous period in that paper's history, with the liberal Swanson shaking Calgary's right-wing establishment to its bones, speeding the city's transition from cowtown to metropolis, and presiding over his fiefdom from a country seat that was a wonder of the foothills country, located on land where, it was said, were written the lines, "Unto the hills about do I lift up my wondering eyes." At least, that is what Swanson said, while quaffing ale from a leather, silver-rimmed beaker that had the name "Oliver Cromwell" engraved on it.

Being a publisher, Swanson became eligible for the fishing trips paper companies lay on for people who buy their product, especially newspapers. In Swanson's day, *The Calgary Herald* was the big money-spinner in the Southam chain and on fat days its presses ate paper by the trainload, so Swanson got invited on a lot of fishing trips.

Years before, in his reporting days, Frank had occasion to call in at the head office of the Canadian Pacific Railway in Montréal's Windsor Station. He was there, as what reporter wasn't, to pick up some of the free transportation that the railways doled out in those days to gentlemen of the press (there were no ladies). The Holy of Holies for freebies was the office of J. Travers Coleman, head of public relations for the C.P.R., a big, jovial man who was a nephew of the president of the railroad, D.C. Coleman.

Behind his desk, Trav Coleman had one of those huge maps of Canada that you used to find in schools and public buildings—the big, roll-down kind that could fill an entire wall, and had Dominion of Canada printed across it in large letters, with every province a different color. Those maps were the same vintage as the ones of the world that had the British Empire parts in red, which gave Canada a position of world dominance, since lost when the red went out of use.

Coleman would greet visitors with the question, "Do you want a river, a mountain, a lake or an island?" Many of the features on the huge map were without names, and when the visitor had made a choice, Coleman would climb up on a stool, pick a spot and write the visitor's name on it. Swanson said he would like an island, and Coleman inked it in, on an unnamed island off the coast of British Columbia.

Swanson got his free rail pass and left, thinking what a clever conversational gimmick Coleman had going with his map.

Decades later, Swanson, as publisher of *The Calgary Herald*, was off on his first big fishing trip as guest of his newsprint supplier. He flew to Vancouver, transferred to a float plane and was flown up the coast to a lake in the mountains where the fishing was said to be fabulous.

Midway through the flight, the pilot of the Beaver turned to Frank and hollered, over the roar of the engine, "Are you Mr. Swanson?"

Frank said yes, he was.

"Well," said the pilot, "you may be interested to know that we are just passing over Swanson Island."

Frank flipped, and asked to see the map.

"It's not printed on there because it's so small," said the pilot, "but that's what we always call it."

Swanson never did find out what happened to Coleman's map, but became convinced there were forces at work that were beyond understanding.

The fishing, incidentally, was great—rainbows galore, for publishers only—Frank went every year until he retired and lost the *Calgary Herald* franchise. As Allan Fotheringham once rightly said, there are only two jobs worth having on a paper, columnist and publisher. Except, he might have added, columnists don't get invited to fish by paper-makers.

For a newspaperman, Swanson was unusual, in that he had more friends outside the news business than inside, and this stood him in good stead when he became a publisher, since publishers are supposed to ingratiate themselves into the business and social communities of the cities to which they are assigned, and in the case of the Southam papers, there are handbooks to guide new publishers on who's who locally, with the accent on the Big Advertisers.

Before reaching these heights, Frank favored friends who had shared his combat experience in war, and one of these was Colonel Charles Petch, the only Canadian to have a street in Normandy named after him—Boulevard Lieutenant Colonel Charles Petch, in the Normandy village of Authie, where Col. Petch's battalion fought one of the fiercest of the invasion battles.

Petch, like Swanson, became an avid trout fisherman after the war, and both frequented a table of storytellers in Ottawa's Rideau Club, where the subject frequently turned to trout. Petch's prize was a six-and-a-half-pound speckled, so impressive that he had it mounted in a magnificent glass case, which he bequeathed to the Rideau Club, where it now has pride of place in the main bar, having been hung there when the membership voted against a traditional barroom nude.

Another of Petch and Swanson's fishing buddies was showing the fish to a female companion and marvelling at its size, saying, "If I'd caught a fish like that, I'd mount it, too."

Whereupon the woman uttered what ranks as one of the snappiest comebacks in club history, to the delight of all in the bar who heard it. "You'd mount a water spider, if you could get its legs apart!"

THE PRIME MINISTER

I n the business of power fishing, there are those who care about power, and those who care about fishing. Brian Mulroney falls somewhere in between. He differs from others we've been talking to in two respects: he was more often a host than a guest on fishing trips, and he has always enjoyed fishing trout more than salmon.

What made Mulroney a fishing host was his job as president of the Iron Ore Company of Canada. It is a rare president of any major Canadian company who does not have at least one fishing lodge at his command, and Mulroney had three, providing a range of fishing from speckled trout through Atlantic salmon.

Photographs of the parties he invited to the camps show men who became prominent in the political life of the country, an indication that the political life was never far from Mulroney's mind. In those days, he was the most gregarious of men, and he might still be, but for the rival claims on his time of politics and family. When he talks of fishing it is with fond recollection, but it has more to do with poker games and story-telling in smoke-filled cabins than with battles on the fabled Québec waters he controlled. When he talks about his sidekick, Pat MacAdam, his eyes gleam, and it's all about the time MacAdam got on a story-telling roll and talked for three days and nights without repeating a yarn, leaving everybody aching from laughter.

Mulroney says the Iron Ore camps were available not only to executives of the company, but to friends and suppliers, and hourly employees had the privilege of drawing lots for salmon fishing on the Sainte-Marguerite or fishing at the two trout camps. (Iron Ore shared the Marguerite with Alcan.)

"North Camp, up beyond Schefferville, was for the real skilled fishermen," says the prime minister, "but I stuck with Kurbidot because it was the easiest fishing for trout. I fished on the Jupiter for salmon for a couple of days, a number of years. Picture Paul Martin [Junior] and I out together fishing on the Jupiter River ten years ago.

"I loved the salmon fishing, but I acquired the taste that I do have for trout fishing from my father in Baie Comeau. I used to go trout fishing with him north of Baie Comeau, and he was a great trout fisherman. I never was, but I kind of enjoyed the fact that we always came back with something when he went trout fishing. It was in Lake LaLutre, north of Baie Comeau, fly fishing. There wasn't much fishing for many years after I left home, but when I came to the Iron Ore Company I re-acquired the taste for trout, and I'd go twice a year, every year, and bring old friends up, flying from Montréal to Labrador City and taking float planes to Lake Kurbidot, about half an hour south into Québec."

Mulroney has a way of seeming to care about nobody except the person he is speaking to, and nothing but the subject under discussion, so he was sounding like a confirmed angler until he laughed.

"I'm nothing like Simon and Jake," he said, adding that he had fished with them both. He added that it was hard to be a head of government and find time for fishing, but then he laughed again.

"The man you want to talk to is George Bush—he's crazy about fishing," said Mulroney. "I've been out with him at least three times at Kennebunkport, and we haven't done badly at all. George will fish every chance he gets and he never seems to get tired of it." Why hadn't Mulroney invited Bush to fish Québec waters for the salmon or trout, or at least drop a line in Harrington Lake? Never enough time, was the not-too-convincing answer—maybe Mulroney was keeping the fishing as Canada's ace-in-the-hole when negotiating got tough.

Back to Iron Ore, and Lake Kurbidc.

"The guides knew where the fish were, and we would fly on float planes the ten or fifteen minutes to the hot spots, especially the rapids between lakes. The guides would line us up on opposite sides of the fast water, and we would fish there for a couple of hours if we did well. If not, they'd say to move— there were canoes stashed all over the place. Along about noon, we would all get together and they'd bring beans and bread and we would cook the trout and sit on the rocks. The lunches were always the best part of it, fish right off the fire, home-made baked beans that they would bring, home-made bread, and that would lead to story-telling and a lot of good fun."

After lunch, they would go back at it until late in the afternoon, when the planes started flying the anglers home to the main camp. That night, more trout for dinner, and then the social evening.

Wheeling and dealing?

"Well," said Mulroney, "these were associates, and friends. John Robarts came up, Frank Moores, Dalton Camp, Findlay MacDonald. I think people read more into the politics than we really talked about. It wasn't just a bunch of Conservatives, there were lots of Liberals, and it was good to put up your feet with the bunch. Even the jokes sound better. It wasn't designed to talk business."

Other parties were different. Mulroney recalls that when the treasurer of Iron Ore, Van Holden, would bring business associates and suppliers, they would talk about the future of the company.

At camp in 1981, Senator John Lynch Staunton, United Nations Ambassador Yves Fortier, Québec M.N.A. Richard Holden, Prime Minister Mulroney, Senior Advisor Arthur Campeau, and two guides.

"I didn't do that," says Mulroney. "I brought friends and associates of various kinds. We might have talked about who was going to win the next election. We played poker every night and the drinkers had a field day. There were prizes for the most caught and the largest fish. Jim McGrath won once, because one of the participants, the mayor of Pembroke, Ontario, Terry McCann, who was a classmate of mine at college, claimed the biggest trout but, when they were weighed, McGrath won by half a pound. Only the next day did he tell McCann he had stuffed his fish with pebbles." McGrath, who subsequently was named by Mulroney to be Lieutenant Governor of Newfoundland, gave the trophy back. The overweight trout story may, Mulroney thinks, have been the inspiration for a similar incident recounted by Mordecai Richler in his novel, *Solomon Gursky Was Here*.

These days, at Harrington Lake, Mulroney takes the kids out now and then for the evening fishing, and the occasional guest gets a crack at it, including hockey star Bobby Orr.

How does he rate the fishing?

"It's good, but not like The Labrador."

What is, though? What was the biggest fish Mulroney had ever caught?

"It was a salmon, on the Jupiter, about fourteen pounds. I've seen much bigger than that. I always caught my limit on the Jupiter, but didn't do well on size.

"On trout, it was not unusual for others to get speckles of four-and-a-half or five pounds. That's a big trout—you could hardly lift a string of them after a good catch. Not all days were exciting, but a lot of them were, out there with not a soul within hundreds and hundreds of miles."

Today?

"I get lots of invitations, but I just don't have the opportunity. I try to stick very close to home with the kids."

Any other recollections?

"Yes. One evening on a northern lake, we were in our canoes and, crossing the lake, was a whole herd of caribou. We came up to them and were able to pat them on the heads and rub their antlers. Unforgettable."

Thus Mulroney the angler, self-described as "a bit player in the galaxy of fisherman like Simon. An enthusiastic amateur, hooked on other things."

EPILOGUE

E nd of stories.

Back to reality, unless you are one of that happy breed who think the days spent fishing are the real ones, and all the rest are just marking time. The happiest solution is a crossover, when the joys and lessons of angling are applied to the rest of life's activities.

The other night, my younger daughter and her younger daughter appeared at my door, and each of them brought me a trout they had caught. When a man gets a trout from his daughter, and one from his granddaughter, both on the same night, it is a happy thing.

Lac Bernard, Québec
May, 1991